INSPIRABLE

INSPIRABLE

THE GREATEST SKILL OF ALL

DANIEL LAYA

For Sara,

who reminded me I was born Inspirable

Contents

Foreword

When Daniel Laya asked me if I'd like to write a foreword for his book, I jumped at the chance. Why? Because Daniel is truly one of the most inspiring and inspirable people I know — Professor, Entrepreneur, Executive Coach and Consultant, Migrant, Father, Husband, Technologist, Storyteller, Comedian, Photographer, Fitness Enthusiast... I realized that the number of labels I could pin to him, in which he excels, is more than virtually anyone else I know. And more importantly, during our almost decade long friendship, his endless stream of kindness, playfulness, humility and authenticity has sustained every conversation we've had so that ideas, actions and friendship have advanced every time.

If Inspirable, as Daniel writes, "is the capacity to make yourself more permeable to the positive behaviors of those with whom you connect," then what you hold here in your hands is a manual from a master who has not only walked the path, but created and signposted it for others.

In this book, I believe Daniel has done what few experts ever manage to do — to see themselves plus others like them from the balcony, and to objectively codify the attitudes, habits and approaches that make them stand out. And then to explain it all through stories, real-world examples and exercises that will engage you from one page to the next.

I think we live in an age where inspirability is more needed than ever. Where technological advances are replacing traditional human work at a breakneck pace. Where the world's balance of power is shifting from the global north to the BRIC countries.

Where polarization and division are used as raw fuel for attention, airtime and mindshare.

In this new era, being adaptive, positive and always-learning is a way that undoubtedly leads to greater success and peace of mind, whether you're a startup CEO, a Parent or a Priest. In a world of growing change, discord and uncertainty, only the most inspirable will experience sustained joy, health and prosperity.

Treat this book as a personal plan: map your InQ against the five sections of the Inspirable Way and visualize yourself to become more productive, vital and transformative. Re-examine and nurture your Tribe to create a vibrant system around you that brings you outsized intelligence, insights and connections. Tweak your Context to remove the invisible friction in your life. Take action. Measure your progress against where you started from.

And know that you can do it. You truly can. As Daniel says, each of us was born inspirable!

I sincerely hope you enjoy your transition from where you are now to a newer, more consciously inspirable way of living.

Haider Imam, September 2022

Author 'Straight to Yes' (Wiley, 2013)

Co-founder Tao Leadership and culturbook.io

Partner, Ernst & Young

Introduction - The Greatest Skill of All

Lewis was born in Delaware, Ohio, on the 16th of March 1983, and since his early childhood he wanted to become an All-American athlete[1]. By the time he left for college, Lewis was almost 6.5 feet tall and passionate about playing football. He had an opportunity to play at different universities, including Ohio State. When Lewis got to his fourth year, his dream had come true, although not in the way he expected it. He became an All-American athlete in a discipline he never trained for: decathlon!

The following year, he did become an All-American football athlete, but something was not right. Suddenly, he had lost all the excitement. His recent achievements were no longer enough, and although he was obsessed with becoming a professional player, he lacked the enthusiasm from before.

Suddenly, tragedy knocked on his door. His father, who was his best friend and coach, was involved in a car accident that left him in a coma for three months. His father never fully recovered from it, leaving Lewis heartbroken.

After that, Lewis got picked to play in an arena football league team but he played only one year - He had to quit because of a career-ending injury. This sequence of events left a 24-year-old

---

[1] According to Brittanica.com: "All-America team, an honorific title given to outstanding U.S. athletes in a specific sport in a given year competing at the collegiate and secondary school levels. Originally the term referred to a select group of college gridiron football players. Athletes selected to an All-America team are known as All-Americans."

Lewis broke, depressed, and sleeping on his sister's couch because he could not afford a place to live. He needed to find a way out of his terrible situation.

As his dad could no longer help him, he started connecting with high-profile business professionals and business owners to learn from their success stories. These conversations lit the spark again inside Lewis. He realized that his obsession with selfish, short-term goals was not doing him any favors. He needed to focus on a greater purpose to be better, and he wanted to share his experience with others.

In 2013, Lewis created a podcast. He did his first interview using his mobile phone. Only one person was listening to the show. He called his podcast "The School of Greatness".

After 10 years and with more than 1,000 episodes, Lewis has interviewed some of the most influential people in the world. The show has been downloaded more than 150 million times, covering topics like fitness, money, nutrition, spirituality, entrepreneurship, mental health, and human rights. Lewis was recognized by President Barack Obama as one of the top 100 entrepreneurs under 30 years old. He has been featured in The New York Times, Forbes, ESPN, Sports Illustrated, and many other media giants.

I started listening to Lewis Howes through The School of Greatness several years ago, and I still do every week. I was enchanted by the fascinating people he interviewed in each episode, but I also remember thinking and mentioning to my wife that I really liked Lewis because he was not trying to be the star of the show, as many interviewers do. Instead, he was just asking the right questions so his guests could talk about the subjects that were most appealing to the show's audience.

During the discussions, Lewis frequently shared with his listeners the difficult moments in his life. His vulnerability made me feel like I knew him well after listening to hundreds of episodes, although I have never formally met him.

One day I realized what really fascinated me about Lewis Howes: He was learning something in every episode and it showed. He had the skill of letting every guest amaze him. One word came to my mind: **inspirable**.

After this epiphany, a storm of ideas took shape in my head. Understanding how people develop and what inspires them to grow has been my obsession for decades. While leading human resources departments in multinational companies or working as an executive coach, I have supported the development of many people in Latin America, Europe, and the Middle East. However, year after year, I asked myself the same question: If personal development is so beneficial for the individual, why does it have to be so hard?

The reason is that current personal development options, especially those dedicated to producing a change in mindset, beliefs, or values, also provide quite a lonely journey. It requires a lot of willpower to achieve your goal, and if you fail, your lack of commitment is to blame. This type of personal development follows a structure created 40 to 50 years ago, and most alternative methods still don't deviate far from this model.

The real personal development solution lies in what Howes does in every episode of The School of Greatness: connecting with people who could inspire.

What Does It Mean to be Inspirable?

I had to create this concept myself, as I found nothing similar in my research[2]. Inspirable is *the capacity to make yourself more permeable to the positive behaviors of those with whom you connect.*

When you hear a beautiful piece of music that you haven't heard before and it moves you in some way, you are open to receiving the notes, the piano crescendos, diminuendos, and the tempo. However, you need to have your ears and heart open to this experience; nothing can inspire you if you are not inspirable.

Inspirable people can overcome stagnate beliefs, update their personal habits, and begin business practices with open minds. In practical terms, an inspirable person can easily emulate habits from their meaningful connections to improve their health, wellbeing, relationships, professional and leadership skills, work-life balance, time management, emotional intelligence, and many other areas.

However, I have good news and bad news for you. The good news is, every one of us is born inspirable. As a child, I was eager to learn from and emulate my parents, then my teachers, classmates, colleagues, and bosses. The bad news is that many people lose that drive along the way, some earlier than others, depending on their experiences.

In the corporate world, you climb the ladder as a manager or specialist. Then you are accountable for your team's motivation; you have to be their source of inspiration. With your additional responsibilities, you get some interesting perks

---

[2] The Merriam-Webster definition of "Capable of being inspired" is correct but does not shed much light on the subject.

such as business class traveling, a private office, a company car, and company shares. All this sounds tempting, but in the long run, you become isolated in your new role. You get lonely in your own life and then you complain that the world is not what it used to be. You've lost the connection by being the inspirer, not the inspiree.

That's what happened to me. At age 36 I was already burnt out, completely un-inspirable. I was only in contact with people exactly like myself, talking all the time about what would happen if we lost our jobs. We were afraid, and we had reasons to be. We were slowly becoming obsolete.

My job became unbearable and eventually I decided to quit.

After I left the corporate world and became an entrepreneur, I had opportunities to work with many people from different backgrounds, companies, and countries. I became inspired by them. It was then I realized that inspiration is the chief ingredient for change, for dealing with resistance. On top of this, my experience as a business school professor[3], absorbing fresh ideas from my students all the time, drove my inspirable levels through the roof.

You will discover in this book that myself, Lewis Howes, and many others, have been on a journey that began when we were born inspirable. Then, when we joined the workforce, we became inspirational to others. For one reason or another, we lost the skill to be inspirable. Fortunately, after this difficult period, we came back to Consciously Inspirable. It is called consciously because it is a deliberate decision to emerge back.

After this long expedition, I faced an enormous challenge: How can I create a framework to help everyone become inspirable,

---

[3] IE University. https://www.ie.edu/

so they can unlock their dreams just as Lewis and many others have?

To solve this challenge, I used insights from four primary sources:

1. **My personal journey.** There is one thing I loved from every interview that Lewis Howes did in The School of Greatness: His guests talked about their lives, and how their experiences shaped their growth and their contributions to society. This helped me understand the context that produced their ideas and their way of seeing the world. I will do the same here, sharing my successes and failures, and their contribution to my thesis.

2. **My professional journey.** I have dedicated my life to people's development, accumulating intense experiences in many industries and corporations. So, readers must know my proposal is backed up by decades of trying different personal growth approaches.

3. **Research.** Investigations by classic experts in behavioral sciences such as Robin Dunbar and David McClelland, or contemporary ones, like Daniel Kahneman, Frederic Laloux, Charles Kadushin, and others, validate the ideas presented in this book.

4. **Stories of others.** The lives of notable people, being inspired by others and having grown out of anonymity to cause a positive impact in their communities, will illustrate the way to create inspirable organizations and societies.

The result of the combination of these four sources is the Inspirable Way© framework: a five-step cycle that will help you make the best of all those talented people who surround you, so you can grow in a process that is full of excitement.

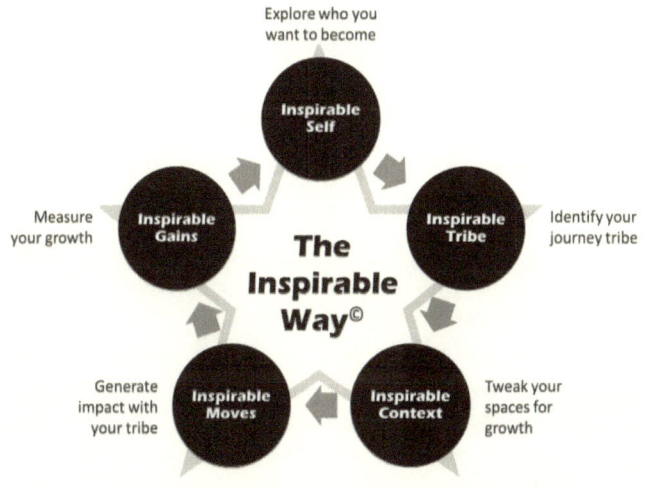

Figure 1: The Inspirable Way

During this exhilarating journey, you will:

- Measure your Inspirable Quotient (InQ) to have a clear starting point.
- Explore what the person you want to be will look like.
- Get closer to the people in your tribe who will inspire you to get there.
- Remove all the obstacles to your development.
- Get your changes to stick and continue to evolve.
- Bring your learnings to your workplace and personal life.
- Understand how to contribute to your organization and your community.

Being inspirable is *the skill* that opens the door to acquiring any other skill and the enabler for your growth beyond your dreams. That's why I like to say: *Inspirable is the greatest skill of all.*

PART I - BORN INSPIRABLE

Chapter 1 - Birth

Understand the context in your early days:

What were your limitations?

Who were sources of inspiration?

We are all born inspirable. As babies, we are naturally ready to learn and soak up everything in our environment. Infants are amazed at the taste of their food, the colors of the screen, the notes in the music dancing around their ears, the touch of the family cat's fur, and the smile of their mom as she picks them up to cuddle.

As they become familiar with these sensations, babies reach for more, constantly putting things into their mouths. It's one way they explore the world, and that's why they love textures. The sense of touch helps them to gain an understanding of things around them. More and more, toddlers actively engage with their environment: responding to voices, figuring out how to hold a spoon, and sounding out the letters in the alphabet, always with the help of their parents or caregivers.

Children are constantly looking for role models to imitate; they learn best by interacting with warm, nurturing, and loving people. Typically, we are inspired first by our parents, then by our grandparents, and maybe an older sibling. As we grow, we might seek mentoring from some of our teachers (hopefully) and older students. There may also be neighbors, aunts, uncles, and people from youth or sports organizations that become a part of the list of people to emulate.

During this part of our lives, we create a pattern for our inspiration: We are conditioned to believe that knowledge and wisdom come from people who are senior to us. This is a blessing in our early development as it makes us imitate "qualified" people but is one of the biggest barriers to becoming inspirable in later stages of life. It holds us back from discovering that people are substantial sources of encouragement and incentive, no matter what generation they come from and whether they are older or younger than us.

This is a story

I wrote this book to share some parts of my life that helped me create The Inspirable Way©. I want you to connect with my successes, failures, strengths, and vulnerabilities so that you can understand why I am proposing this alternative.

I also thought this book would guide you to write your own success story, your growth story, the story where you become inspirable with your meaningful connections.

As a sci-fi lover, I enjoy hero stories, which is why I am shaping this book as a hero story. I love how the structure of these stories makes books more exciting to read. Academic Joseph Campbell coined the most commonly used hero story structure[4] in 1949. It has three acts:

---

[4] Kishore, Kamal. "Joseph Campbell's Hero's Journey". Harappa, March 2021. https://harappa.education/harappa-diaries/joseph-campbell-heros-journey/

- **The Departure Act**. The Hero leaves the Ordinary World because they receive a call to an adventure. There is a strong need to change something in the Hero's life.
- **The Initiation Act.** By venturing into unknown territory, or we could say, outside of the comfort zone, the Hero becomes a staunch champion through various trials and challenges, being trained and developing new skills.
- **The Return Act**. The Hero returns in triumph. In this stage, the Hero demonstrates that, in addition to the goals achieved, they have transformed into a more skilled and mature person.

When I thought about which could be my Departure Act, my childhood seemed like a good starting point to open up. So, time to get cozy as I have a story to tell ...

Familia inspiration

My story starts with my infancy, which was similar to the environment that I described on the previous page: loving family, decent teachers, and mentors. I was fortunate to grow up being inspired by my amazing parents. At that time, my dad was a resourceful, tech and gadget lover person; my mom was the responsible one who did all the family's short-term and long-term planning.

I have to say that my parents were very committed to their children. Wherever my parents went, they took us with them. We were always with them, and they were always there for us.

Education was very important in my family. Our daily lifestyle included lots of learning and reading. Both my parents were English professors, and I was born when they were still very young: My dad was 25, and my mom was 21. When they went to get their master's degrees at Georgetown University in Washington D.C., I was still learning to talk. Instead of learning Spanish, which was supposed to be my mother tongue, I learned English. I picked up Spanish when we moved back to Venezuela, my home country.

My mom raised me to be independent and reliable. During my childhood she taught me how to use the stove to warm up the food she left in the fridge for when I got back from school (they were working all day long). She also taught me to clean up my room; in my early teens this included washing my clothes and ironing my shirts. Besides the operational stuff, the key lesson from my mom was very simple: You can do whatever you want in life, just make sure to pay your bills, don't borrow money or go bankrupt. She advised us to keep the future in mind because everyone gets old and things are going to happen. I am very proud of these values, but I have to say that many times in my life I have confused independence with isolation. Becoming inspirable has been quite a challenge for me, as interdependence and collaboration were not part of my early life core values.

My dad is this imaginative, smart guy. He's not as organized or farsighted in economic terms as my mom, but he's extremely creative. During the writing of this book, I realized my dad has also been the ambassador of joy and optimism in our family, a role that I disregarded my whole life but has become a priority for me as I age.

My father was a gadget lover when I was young. In our home we always had computers, and sometimes I helped him build and sell computers to earn extra income. He didn't have a background in technology; he just could easily learn anything that included an instruction manual[5] (or not). He was passionate

---

[5] We are talking about the 1980s here. The Internet was not available and YouTube tutorials were not even an idea.

about it and loved to involve me in it. My love of technology comes from that time. Some people have negative opinions of tech, but my dad, mom, brother, and I all read science fiction. My dad brought the future we read in books to our home by buying every newly invented gadget. I'm not only talking about computers here but also watches with a radio inside, a portable tv set for the car, and wireless connection to devices using radio frequency. My home was so techie 40 years ago that my parents were able to edit and print their own first book in one of our bedrooms.

I think my relationship with my parents was very beneficial. I keep those two voices in my head frequently, and that balance allows me to plan my life well.

Sometimes situations were tough for my parents, especially with a special needs daughter. My sister, three years younger than me, had problems from birth, so she needed round-the-clock care. She lived for nine years before her health issues took her from us. I know that had to be difficult for my parents, but they made sure she had everything she needed while both of them worked full-time. They grieved deeply afterward, but throughout the heartache, they still had time for my brother and me. There was never anything missing in our lives.

My brother also inherited their inner strength. He is six years younger than me and may be the person who better embodies the word *resilience*[6], especially after he left his psychology studies to chase his passion in a kitchen, fighting his way to become a chef in Ecuador. Our family did not initially support his decision to leave college, but in the end, we surrendered to his persistence and backed him up 100%. Through him, I understood early in life that someone younger could inspire me.

---

[6] Resilience is the capacity to recover quickly from difficulties.

Inspirational Grandad and Grandma

My grandad was also an enormous source of inspiration for me. I still remember going with him to a lake at the park to go rowing. He was also a professor like my parents, and he was always trying to transfer some of his knowledge to me.

"This is fun, Grandpa!" I said, sitting in the boat as a kid at almost 10 years old.

"It's more than just fun, Daniel," he said. "Look at the muscles in your arms. We are not just rowing. We are developing coordination of the mind and muscles." And while we were doing all that, he was teaching me Russian words[7], one of his passions.

The experience itself of going with my grandpa to the park several times and transforming the fun into a learning experience is something that I remember as if it were yesterday.

Grandpa passed away three decades ago, but his values are still present in our lives. Grandpa was the senior guide in the family, the balance. He helped everyone when they needed advice. For his grandchildren, he was a figure of inspiration and respect. Later on in my life, I also became a professor, so teaching is apparently something that runs in the family.

My grandma was a source of inspiration in a different way. Everyone loved her. She didn't have any advice to give, just love, and she was the best listener. It took ages for the corporate world of messianic leaders to realize that listening is one of the

---

[7] My Grandad always talked about Russia, although he never went there. Later in life, I had the opportunity to give a presentation about the future of work in Moscow, and my thoughts before saying my first words were: You would have loved to be here, Grandad!

most important leadership skills, while my grandma was already guiding us along this path.

In many ways, she was ahead of her time. My family came from my grandmother's second marriage. She divorced when she was twenty-something in the 1940s. I don't think divorce was a very common thing anywhere in the world by then, so hers was pretty unusual; maybe taking the less traveled road runs in the family, as well. My grandma remarried later to my grandad (marrying a divorced woman might have been even less common at the time) and founded our family, which included the children of my grandma's previous marriage. She was the string that tied everything together with her love. She treated us all equally with her patience and attention as we spoke to her.

I have always thought of my grandma as my favorite person in the world, but I never knew why. Now, long after she's gone, I realize that her joyful existence will be one of my beacons in this new stage of my life.

Out there too soon

I started university when I was 16, very young in comparison with my classmates. This was because, in my early childhood, my parents and teachers saw I could do a lot of things early, so they thought it to be a good idea to jump me ahead to a higher grade. At that time, the criteria were based more on my reading and math skills than on my emotional maturity. The result was I was always at a disadvantage in comparison with my classmates. If my male friends saw me as a kid, can you imagine what the girls in my class thought of me? They saw me as a pet.

It seemed like a nightmare to me. I see my daughter, who is one of the eldest in her class, I realize how comfortable she is in her environment. This was something I didn't have as the youngest in my grade.

However, there was one positive aspect of being the class pet: I was never alone. I was always close to someone who could protect me from the typical bullies. My friend list included some of the big guys in high school and college.

I was never brilliant at school or university. I hated to memorize so much stuff without understanding what was it for, and if you were not good at learning by rote, it was impossible to get the best grades.

Things changed when I started college with a major in human resources. The boring learning by heart was still there in most of the subjects, but others were very practical, such as understanding labor law, how to set salaries, recruitment, workforce costs, economics, and information technology. Also, there were some professors that made the difference, who I refer to as the storytellers. Those who wanted everyone to understand the purpose of the class and to engage brought all the excitement I could only find in books. Participating in class seems like a no brainier nowadays, but Generation X and Baby Boomers reading this book will agree that it was not common at all in our times. In most lectures, information was flowing only in one direction.

I was definitely more attracted to the content in college but still struggled with some boring subjects that I either failed because I did not study enough or passed by cheating on the tests. Then a new kind of subjects came up, those that were too difficult for me: statistics and economics. Though these classes were taught by some of the best professors, I just didn't get it. I ended up having to repeat one year in college, and even after that, I was still among the youngest in my class. After assuming that failing was not the end of the world, I felt way more comfortable.

Economics, math, and statistics became my favorite subjects and part of my comfort zone from that year onward.

When I started studying for my master's degree in economics, the material was even better, more about the real world. The relationships with the professors were closer and class groups were smaller. I failed many times, but by then it was all about learning and being inspired by some professors that I considered geniuses as well as the other students in my class who were also brilliant.

One last funny story: I finished my master's degree and the only thing I had left to graduate was to deliver the final project. By then I was already working with the AES Corporation, starting one of the most interesting projects in my working life. I had no time for academic stuff, and I said to myself: I'll deliver it later that year. Although I never delivered it, I have no regrets, I got all the inspiration I needed.

Chapter Insights

This chapter is about the beginning of my journey, but it is also about yours. I am sharing with you the context where I was born and raised so that you can understand the limitations that I faced and the possibilities that I had. I want you to stay active during the entire book, so when I share something about myself, think about your story: Did you face something similar or different?

In this period of my life, three elements shaped the way I saw the world:

1. Having a supporting family where many members were teachers or professors, so *learning was a valued skill*.

2. Besides being the first-born child, in many social circles where I belonged, I was usually the youngest. *This made me try harder than the rest or give up quicker.* Because of suffering occasional bullying, I was quick to get allies, but it was difficult for me to trust others.

3. Born in a family of science-fiction readers *made me think about the future as the place where I want to be.*

If you are to become inspirable, it is interesting to take a quick trip back in time to when you were a child.

- Who were your sources of inspiration? Why?
- How did they operate: by themselves or in collaboration with others?
- How did your context define your most important traits?

Chapter 2 - The concept

What's the relation between inspiration and creativity?

How is this different than admiration?

What does it have to do with bonding?

Inspirable is the capacity to make yourself more permeable to the positive behaviors of those with whom you connect.

This is the concept I came up with during a moment of inspiration in the middle of the COVID-19 lockdown in Madrid. Its push was so strong and so constant that it provided me with the incentive to write this book. But after my epiphany, when I started talking about it with friends and colleagues, I realized this concept could be confused with others, such as inspiration, creativity, and admiration. So, let's start by talking about what being inspirable is not.

It is not about inspiration

It is not about having inspiration or being inspired. Inspiration is a stage or a moment, while being inspirable is a skill that will constantly keep you open to inspiration. According to Jesús

Alcoba[8], one of the few modern researchers of inspiration, you cannot make inspiration happen; you cannot control when or where because it is spontaneous. This book is not a method to get inspired. This is a book to become inspirable, meaning *being open to many sources of inspiration*.

What kind of inspiration am I talking about here? The one that generates a behavior that improves who you are, aligned to who you really want to be.

I'm definitely not talking here about Archimedes' famous Eureka moment[9] while lying in a bathtub where he discovered a way to calculate the volume of irregular objects by measuring the volume of water displaced by his body in the bathtub, or Isaac Newton when an apple falling from a tree landed on his head and facilitated the ideas to write his universal laws of gravitation. These are *internal inspirations*, ideas that seem to come out of nowhere while you are waiting for the bus or taking a shower. They might be the product of your subconscious processing of all the ideas you have accumulated about a certain subject or just your memory retrieving a forgotten experience.

This is more about being permeable to external inspirations, those coming from the people in your environment: your home, your workplace, your yoga group. It is not about masterpieces either. It is about small achievements that derivate into big personal transformations. Archimedes and Newton's main objective was to solve *one problem*. This is not a book to assist you in solving problems; this is a book to help you transform yourself, which will help you solve *many problems*.

---

[8] Jesús Alcoba, *Inspiración: La llama que enciende el alma*. (Madrid: Alianza Editorial, 2017.)

[9] "Eureka Effect." Wikipedia. June 21, 2022.
https://en.wikipedia.org/w/index.php?title=Eureka_effect&oldid=1094171665

This is more about the group of friends that create a running club to be healthier and after that, are constantly possessed by the energy that generates them being together, learning together, and, as a secondary effect, achieving together.

This is about grad students who join a business school to improve their knowledge, but as their connections get stronger, they get so much more. Becoming inspirable, they absorb business acumen, incorporate better health practices, and improve their connection with different cultures. *Inspiration is temporary. Inspirable is a way of life.*

It is not about creativity

Defining creativity is a hard task, and picking one definition from the thousands available is also daunting. Some descriptions can be very complex, and I personally love simplicity. Jesús Alcoba defines creativity as "the capacity to generate something new, using known elements to solve a problem."

Inspiration lives in the world of ideas, and creativity in the world of execution, of tasks and actions. Creativity brings to real life a concept that was born through inspiration. So, you cannot be creative if you don't have a source of inspiration, and you cannot have creativity if you are not inspirable.

Hungarian-American psychologist Mihaly Csikszentmihalyi[10] distinguishes two types of creativity, the Big C and the Small C.

---

[10] Mihaly Csikszentmihalyi, *Creativity: The Psychology of Discovery and Invention.* (New York: Harper Perennial, 2013.)

The Big C is the creativity that transforms culture and the way people transform the world. It is a breakthrough type of thinking. He also calls it Public Creativity, Archimedes and Newton's examples belong here.

Small C is the creativity inspired by our surroundings: the podcasts we listen to, the books we read, and the conversations we have. When you are talking to a friend about a problem and suddenly the argument activates an idea in your mind that could improve the situation, we are talking Small C.

People need big doses of Small C to incorporate the positive behaviors they constantly see around them, but they need to be permeable first.

It is not about admiration

Admiration is passive. You admire Adele's singing from the TV in your living room, but this doesn't make you jump off the couch and start taking singing lessons. Watching Rafael Nadal win his 22nd tennis Grand Slam made you cry with excitement, but it was not the reason you started playing again. In fact, seeing your neighbor go out and play on weekends did the trick. Because of conversations with colleagues you respect, you started improving your leadership skills to get your team engaged; you did not get this push by watching Steve Jobs or Elon Musk on YouTube.

So, now that it is clear what it is not like to be inspirable, let's talk about what this concept is really about.

Inspirable is about bonding

Seeing people who you relate to, just normal people facing many challenges, is what gets you off the couch and imitate them. It makes you inspirable because they have shown how ordinary people can transform themselves. You create bonds with the people you would love to get closer to, those you want to keep in your life. *This differs completely from networking*, which is just getting closer to others for the sake of mutual convenience and usually with a concrete objective in mind, such as closing a sale or obtaining information.

It is about joy

Another big difference with networking is the emotional boost you get when you are inspirable. There is this irrational rush of energy that flows through your body every time you think about that person or group of people who inspires you. They are the ones who make your most difficult projects feel like exciting challenges rather than unbearable workloads.

It is about a having a beginner's mind

Shoshin (初心) is a word from Zen Buddhism meaning "beginner's mind". It is about dropping our expectations and preconceived ideas and seeing the world with an open mind and fresh eyes, like a beginner. In the book *Zen Mind, Beginner's Mind* by Zen teacher Shunryu Suzuki, he outlines the framework behind Shoshin, noting "in the beginner's mind there are many possibilities, in the expert's mind there are few."[11]

The inspirable person has a beginner's mind, and is permeable and eager to learn. Suzuki says that joy[12] can be found with this mindset, and joy is at the core of the Inspirable Way©.

It is the best option

Picture yourself wanting for a while to improve in something, such as learning Japanese. Imagine three scenarios:

- You will join a class with a dedicated professor.
- You will join the same class with a group of people from the office, most of which don't seem interesting at all.
- You will join the same class along with three of the most interesting people you know.

I would say that option 3 is the one most likely to succeed. You will learn the language, create a firm commitment to enrich your life, and you will take a joyful journey.

There will be plenty of achievements in this journey you have already started. You just have to stay focused on your main purpose: Becoming Inspirable.

Become Inspirable

Be Inspirable

---

[11] Shunryu Suzuki, *Zen Mind, Beginner's Mind: Informal Talks on Zen Meditation and Practice*. (Boston: Shambhala Publications, 2006.)

[12] Leo Babauta. "Approaching Life with Beginner's Mind". zen habits. January 27, 2017. https://zenhabits.net/beginner/

Be In

In this book, I will use the phrase "*Be In*" every time I need you to write some thoughts or perform certain actions. The purpose of this is to keep you progressing gently on every page. Let's start.

Be In
Write one activity that you did with others that transformed your view of the task because of the inspiration everyone brought to your group.
_____
_____
_____
_____
_____
_____
_____

Chapter Insights

It is very important to understand at the beginning of the journey what being inspirable is not. We explored the fundamental differences between inspiration, creativity, and admiration. We usually relate these three concepts to colossal achievements and great inventions: Shakespeare, Marie Curie, and Picasso.

- This book is not a guide to achieving great stuff. I will not tell you to "be more ambitious, aim for the stars" because this temporary motivation will just make you feel depressed and guilty for abandoning your quest for change the very next day.

- This is about constantly introducing slight changes in your life that will get you closer to the person you want to be.

The best way to implement these minor adjustments is to be in contact with others who have done it or are doing it. *You'll have to be inspirable to let them inspire you.*

In the next chapter, I will share some experiences from my professional life where being inspirable was the key to my growth from junior positions to management ones.

Chapter 3 - Learning together

Working together in transformation projects creates strong bonds

Being permeable to senior people speeds up growth

Taking risks early in your professional life definitely pays off

As mentioned in the previous chapter, being inspirable is not something you can be by yourself; in fact, it only works when there are others involved. I've had many friends who I've worked side-by-side with to achieve common goals, and the experiences were incredible. However, teamwork is one thing, and becoming inspirable is another. Teamwork is more based on coordination, collaboration, and idea-sharing, while becoming inspirable is about *mirroring the best behaviors of each other to become better human beings*.

In this chapter, I will share some of my life experiences to illustrate times when I was inspirable. It seemed just like normal life to me, so I think I took this ability for granted. The first time I realized the importance of being inspirable was when I lost this valuable skill.

Inspiration by friendship

Alejandro was my doubles tennis partner when we were teenagers. He was a good sports partner and a great friend.

In year 1994, when we were just 20 years old, we started mountain biking and created a website about it just for fun. In that decade, most Internet start-ups were just content portals, and we received an offer from a big one to be part of their website. It was a great opportunity but it was very difficult to implement in practical terms. We were still studying and did not have time to comply with all the requirements they had. Also, we got a little scared of all the legal stuff involved. This was still just a hobby for us and we didn't feel like we knew enough to move forward with it. *We loved technology but we were not entrepreneurs.* We were both raised by parents who worked 9-to-5 jobs, so we didn't know about taking risks. After two days of back-and-forth discussion, we declined the offer.

After this decision, we both continued our lives the traditional way: studying and finding jobs in our fields of expertise. Alejandro became an engineer and started working for an oil company. I became a human resources specialist and took a job at a dairy company. (By the way, it was Alejandro's dad who helped me get that first job.)

Sometimes I looked back with some curiosity: What would have happened if we had said yes? Would we have become the Latino versions of Mark Zuckerberg or just enjoy a few months of decent pay?

When I let my thoughts go back in time, I ask myself, what did we need then to take the risk and go ahead with the proposal? For many years I couldn't find an answer, but now it's clear in my mind: *We needed a bigger, stronger tribe to support us.*

Suit and tie empowerment

I was 21, just after rejecting my first proposal to create a mountain biking start-up, and I got my first job in HR at an Italian dairy products multinational company. It was a fantastic opportunity for someone so young and it was exciting to start wearing a suit and tie.

It was a positive experience. I was valued and supported by my manager, who also took the time to share many things about HR practices like salaries, benefits, administration, and recruitment. I think being taught rather than inspired was more important at that stage of my career, and I felt empowered.

They also hired my lifetime friend Daniel. He was my first partner in the professional world. Our lives together for the past 30 years have been all about inspiring and challenging each other all the time. We met in college and have shared enjoyable moments in life, the inspirable ones and some difficult ones, as well.

At that first job, we worked together for about a year and a half in a 2-x-2-meter cubicle. We did all our work in our cell, I mean cubicle, talking to each other all day. We continuously joked about the resemblance our daily lives had with the story of Richard Gere's movie *Sommersby*[13], where two cellmates get to know so much about each other's lives that when one dies, the surviving one goes back to his family and pretends to be him.

When we started working and saw that most procedures were manual, involving typewriters and carbon paper, we decided we needed to automatize some processes in HR. This was 1996, and there were only about 20 computers in the eight-story

---

[13] "Sommersby". Wikipedia. May 25, 2022.
https://en.wikipedia.org/wiki/Sommersby

building, one of which was in our cubicle. We created the first role profile database in Microsoft Access, and we also automatized the employee transfer procedure.

It was a solid project and just a bit ahead of its time: No one except us could use it, and it would be three more years before the rest of the employees were given computers to work on. However, it was the product of mutual inspiration between Daniel and me to believe that we could have an impact in our workplaces and contribute to the Human Resources function transformation. I also have to give credit to our boss back then, Minerva, who provided the support, the resources, and the guidance to complete it successfully.

Be In

It is easier to become inspirable when you lead or are part of an ambitious project. Write any interesting project or initiative that you led or were part of.

_____

_____

_____

_____

_____

_____

_____

_____

Super Senior Consultants arrive

My next job was also in the HR department, this time for a utilities company. I enjoyed working in the compensation and benefits area, but the most interesting thing was that the company was going through an amazing transformation process.

The project transformation team was composed of a brilliant mix of super senior consultants charging a hefty fee, a talented group of middle managers, and us, a bunch of junior women and men, mostly recruited from my college. The company invested big time to train the people in the transformation team, and I have to say we enjoyed the benefits of this world-class education.

I had a couple of special partners on this part of the journey. My friend Daniel, who also moved to work in the same company, and Ginette, our young, confident boss who was just a few years older than us. She gave us two invaluable things:

- First, we got all the freedom in the world to propose and execute whatever came to our minds.
- Second, she shared her understanding of how organizations work, their processes, politics, the importance of influence, and how to connect the needs of employees and company executives.

Executive coaching

Ginette also signed me up for the most impactful training in my career: becoming an executive coach directly from one of the most influential coaches in the Spanish-speaking world, Rafael Echeverria[14].

For six months, I was part of a coaching training with many people twice my age. One of the most important lessons I received from the experience was the importance of supporting others, as a coach, as a peer, or as a leader. For a 25-year-old guy, this was also a crash course on the basics of leadership: listening, feedback, goal setting, motivation, and empathy. The course included theoretical classes and practical experiences, so I had to coach others to earn the certification, which was a beautiful experience because I coached people who were significantly older than me. I'm sure I helped them, but I also learned big time from their kindness.

From the conceptual perspective, Mr. Echeverria, a philosopher and sociologist, introduced one of the biggest mindset changes that I've experienced. He said: "We don't see the world as it is, we see the world as we are," meaning everyone is perceiving the world according to their own previous experiences and limitations. Echeverria did not coin this phrase, but he was the first person I heard it from. After this, my thinking was never the same. I now understood what empathy meant, and I would use it from then onward in my roles in HR, but also in the jobs I had in the marketing and customer care departments.

The case of the missing HR department

The company I worked for was acquired by an American multinational, AES Corporation, which brought in a whole new

---

[14] Rafael Echeverría. *Ontología del lenguaje*. (Santiago: Ediciones Granica S.A., 2016.)

set of ways of working. Their motto: "We do not need an HR department; our leaders are capable of making the decisions related to people."

The company operated successfully without HR, and this was so uncommon that a Stanford case study was written about it. It was called "Human Resources at AES Corp: The Case of the Missing Department."[15]

The company was also famous because of its company culture, so much so that it was part of a case study by Frederic Laloux. The AES way of working is included in his book *Reinventing Organizations*[16], which became a reference for effective decision-making process.

After AES acquired the company, it started downsizing immediately. They offered me a very good severance package if I decided to leave since there no longer would not be an HR department. But they also gave me the option to stay in a commercial business unit if I wanted, so I continued in the company because if there was an organization that did not need an HR department, *I needed to know what their operations looked like!*

I stayed for six more years, working with professionals that had very different backgrounds from the ones I was used to working within HR. The team I belonged to was composed of engineers, financial wizards, sales experts, and customer care representatives. It was an invaluable experience.

As I continued to work at AES, I became a manager and encountered many learning experiences and opportunities.

---

[15] Jeffrey Pfeffer. "Human Resources at the AES Corporation: The Case of the Missing Department." Stanford Graduate School of Business, 1997.
[16] Frederic Laloux and Ken Wilber. *Reinventing Organizations: A Guide to Creating Organizations Inspired by the Next Stage in Human Consciousness.* (Brussels: Nelson Parker, 2014.)

While I was still in the heights of being inspirable, new challenges would arise.

Be In

Write the names of prospective partners in crime for interesting projects in the future. Spoiler alert: You are going to need this.

_____

_____

_____

_____

_____

_____

_____

_____

Chapter Insights

I have shared in this chapter three very different experiences where being inspirable was key to my development:

- First, automatizing HR processes with my longtime friend Daniel. Working side-by-side, every problem each of us faced was a problem for both. We worked under the belief that we were improving the efficiency of our department and also developing great technical skills for the future.
- Second, being permeable to my boss Ginette's seniority and with the enormous boost of the coaching training that she offered to me, I developed a deeper understanding of how organizations work and an initial soft skills set.

- Third, as an HR professional, I took the risk of working in a company that did not need an HR department to operate. Interacting with professionals from different functions, I could identify my core skills and put them into action. I was not tied to HR anymore, but I knew my people skills were key to any organization.

Chapter 4 - Not IQ but InQ, the Inspirable Quotient

How inspirable you are?

How do you measure being inspirable?

Hints on how to grow your InQ

Let's make being inspirable something tangible. I invite you to calculate your Inspirable Quotient (InQ). It will take you about 10-15 minutes maximum. The sole purpose of this test is to make you aware of your current situation and to help you track your progress as you become more inspirable. It is not a tool to compare yourself with others, neither by design nor intention.

I have grouped the questions using the 5 components of The Inspirable Way© model, which I will extensively explain in Chapter 7. In the following segment, you will read the analysis of your results by section.

You'll have five groups of questions, three questions in each, for 15 questions in total.

Respond to each of the questions with scores from 0 to 3 and add your results in each section of the table.

0=Never **1 = Rarely** **2 = Sometimes** **3 = Usually**

How frequently...	Scores (0-3)
You identify your main areas of development.	
You define and review the vision of your future.	
You check the status of your priorities: sleep, food, exercise, work.	
A. Inspirable Self score	**Sum A =**
You think you could do better if you collaborate more with others.	
You identify people in your network that inspire you.	
You connect with people who inspire you but are not part of your network.	
B. Inspirable Tribe score	**Sum B =**
You make layout improvements in your home or workspace.	
You listen, read, and watch media aligned with your development needs.	
You realize your environment is affecting your emotional state.	
C. Inspirable Context score	**Sum C =**
You invite people who inspire you to have a chat.	
You create or take part in small groups to perform activities together.	
You create or join large groups with an inspirational purpose.	
D. Inspirable Moves Score	**Sum D =**
You avoid comparing your gains with those of other people or with ideals.	
You are grateful for what you have achieved during the past month.	
You identify the skills you have gained in the past 12 months.	
E. Inspirable Gains Score	**Sum E =**
Total Inspirable Score:	**Average = (A,B,C,D,E)**

Table 1: The Inspirable Quotient questionnaire

Sum up the results of each section, then you can add your results to the radar chart. I have added an example to guide you on how to do it. After this, continue reading to get feedback on your score. If you want to have a reference for your progress, you can respond to the questionnaire again 3 or 6 months later and compare the lines in the chart.

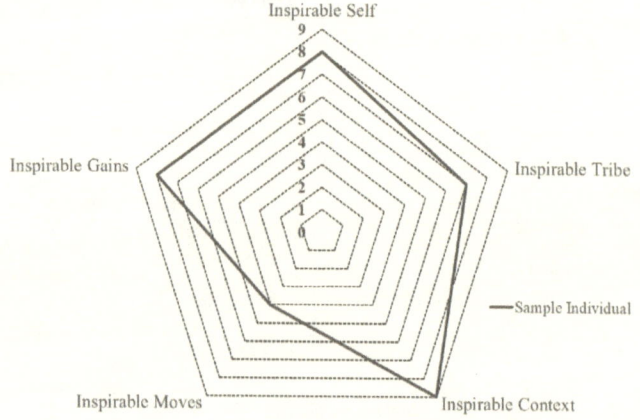

Figure 2: Inspirable Quotient Radar

A. The Inspirable Self section

This area of the questionnaire is about your level of concern for your future self. If your subtotal for this area is 5 or less, it means you are not taking your personal development into your own hands. Maybe you have not reflected recently on who you want to become in the future. The probable causes for this could be endless, but the most common ones are:

- **Cause 1**. You do not have spare time for you to reflect on your future because of your excessive workload, family commitments, or hyper-active social life.

- **Cause 2**. You have delegated consciously or unconsciously your personal development to someone else. Maybe you belong to one of the three major groups of people who do this: The first group delegates it to the company they work for, which has the downside of focusing only on your professional side and your area of specialization. The second group appoints their spouse, partner, or a close friend to define the direction of their growth. This is very common in couples where only one person works. Here could either be the person who is working and making the development decisions or the person who is not working, taking care of the family and house. The third group is the young people who have recently joined the workforce and are focusing more on a short-term career-oriented plan without a holistic personal growth view, or still working with the plans decided by their parents.

- **Cause 3**. You don't think it is useful at this stage in your career to have a personal growth plan. This could be because you think you cannot change who you are, or you are not in the proper mood for this reflection.

If your score for this area was 6 or 7, it means you have thought about your future self and put some plans in place to grow in the professional part, the personal one, or both. However, urgent life situations frequently take priority and you postpone your initiatives. The reasons for this vary a lot, among the most are:

- **Cause 1.** You have thought about how you want your future self to look like, but you are not excited about it or you are still skeptic about the possibility of getting there.

- **Cause 2.** You find it very difficult to make your personal growth priority number one in your life. Frequently, you think you are not being fair to your job, your partner, or your family and it feels selfish.

- **Cause 3.** You know what you want but you are not organized or disciplined enough to make it happen.

If you got 8 or 9 as a result, congratulations! You have a clear idea of who you want to become, feel excited about it, and, even if you don't have a solid action plan, most of your day-to-day behaviors are consistent with this aim. You could benefit from a more structured approach that helps you go beyond where you are now. In Chapter 8, you will see how.

B. The Inspirable Tribe section

This part of the test refers to how much value you assign to the people around you as levers for your growth. If your subtotal for this area is 5 or less, it means that you are not consciously managing your network. You likely have a powerful network, but you have not been able to differentiate who is there just to coordinate actions and who are the ones who bring inspiration to your life and make you want to go beyond your current boundaries.

As in the previous section, this low score could happen for several reasons. The ones I've observed more often are:

- Maybe you have not explored which kind of person you would like to be, so you have not thought about your main areas where you want to grow. If this is the case, you might have gotten a low score in the previous section, as well.
- You have not thought about the type of value each of your acquaintances brings to your life, or you have thought about it but the emotional component makes it difficult to differentiate who inspires you and who doesn't.

If your result for this area is 6 or 7, it means you have clarity on who is who among the people in your close personal and professional circles. You know who is a positive influence for you and who you love spending time with, but you are not good at going beyond those circles and finding inspiration among those you barely know. The reasons for this could be shyness, introversion, fear of rejection, or simply not understanding the size of the prize: the value of strengthening weaker bonds in your network.

If you got a score of 8 or 9, you have defined at least partially the person you would like to be in the future, what are the main development areas that you need to tackle to get there, and who could be the best journey companions.

In the future, you could benefit from an approach that helps you bring more inspirational people into your network and bring those already in it closer to your trust circle. Chapter 10 will provide you with a step-by-step guide for this.

C. Inspirable Context section

The questions in this section of the test measure how much you tweak your context to make it adequate for your aspirations.

If you are getting a score of 5 or less, it is because you are not adjusting your environment to play an active role in your development. By environment, I mean home or workplace layout, content that you watch or listen to, books that you read, and even the type of snacks that you store in your kitchen cabinet.

If you got a score of 6 or 7, it is usually because you do some tweaking here and there, but you still let many distractions coexist in your atmosphere. It is very common that people who start adjusting their context take their first steps in reorganizing their physical environment to make it more efficient. There are other perspectives that need to be included in this equation, because in addition to the physical world, now we coexist in a virtual/digital one. You need to ask yourself, how organized is your digital life? Is it easy for you to find your files, apps, and important information? What kind of content are you exposing yourself to? Is this content helping you get closer to the person you want to be? What emotions does my context trigger in you? How do those emotions contribute to your development journey?

The most common reason for not considering this is because of our lack of awareness of the tremendous impact these details have on our day-to-day lives. I have also observed that in our busy lives, there is a widespread belief that we cannot organize ourselves, and I see more people every day living and accepting chaotic lives. This assumption needs to change.

Congratulations if you got a score of 8 or 9! You are constantly monitoring your context to align it with the person you want to become, and you are reaping the benefits of this behavior.

Always keep in mind that these scores are not an evaluation of yourself; they are just a starting point for your journey to become inspirable. In Chapter 12, you will find a structured approach to make your context work for you in a silent and constant way.

D. Inspirable Moves section

This section provides information about how often you voluntarily take part in activities with others that help you grow closer to the person you want to become.

If your score in this section was 5 or lower, it means you usually avoid participating either in small groups or in larger ones. This might have to do with your personality, as some people prefer small groups for more intimacy, while others tend to rather be in contact with bigger parties. In my case, I prefer starting small initiatives with two or three friends or colleagues, but I also accept invitations to become part of bigger groups if I am aligned with what they are looking for.

Individuals with involvement in a broader range of groups, both small and large, usually get a score of 6 or 7 in this part of the test. This type of person usually has a high level of adaptability. However, it is not common to see people at this level promoting new initiatives themselves. Practical inconveniences could cause this, such as the lack of time or the lack of time management skills, but sometimes is deeper, like not feeling confident enough to reach out to others and introduce your initiative.

If you got a score of 8 or 9, you are not only a participant in a wide variety of groups, but you are also often an initiator. It is not rare to find out that the purpose of the groups you belong to is to become a tribe to gain a new skill or support an important cause. You really hand-pick the initiatives you are going to be part of, thinking: *What will this bring to my development? What can this give to my community?*

In Chapter 14, you will learn how you can intentionally create, promote, or take part in groups that inspire you to become your better self. This will not be a one-size-fits-all approach. You will have many options according to your preferences, personality, and needs.

E. Inspirable Gains section

Is it common that you are satisfied with your weekly achievements or does nothing seem to be enough for you? Do you focus on your own progress or is the progress of others distracting you? Responding to these questions is the purpose of this section.

Getting a score of 5 or less implies you are usually measuring yourself against ideals. This could be goals that someone else sets for you, such as "you need to reach a market share of 30% by year end" or "you need to improve your communication skills." This is very common when working in large companies. However, having objectives set by someone else does not mean you cannot set your own. It is also very common that people with this score compare themselves with their peers all the time. This behavior makes you feel that *no matter how much progress you make, it is never enough.*

If you got a score of 6 or 7, it is because you have been able to set your own objectives. You have taken control of your future. Maybe sometimes you measure against others or against an ideal you, but most of the time you measure your progress against yourself: What have I gained that I did not have last month or last year?

In this area, if you have got a score of 8 or 9, it means most of the time you are not comparing yourself to others, only with yourself. At this level, you are not only focusing on achievements like buying a new home or getting a promotion. Now you are paying special attention to what you are transforming into: more empathic, a better work-life balance, and healthier relations.

In Chapter 15, you will find a simple approach to shift the focus that you have on others, which most of the time leads to frustration, to focus on yourself. Beware: This is not a self-indulgence method. Taking this path will unleash your inner strengths and self-confidence so that you can transform painlessly into the person you want to be.

The Inspirable Quotient

This tool provides you with results per each aspect, and you can easily determine your Inspirable Quotient by calculating the average of the five areas, which should be a number between 0 and 9.

$$InQ = \frac{\Sigma(Self) + \Sigma(Tribe) + \Sigma(Context) + \Sigma(Moves) + \Sigma(Gains)}{5}$$

An InQ example of one of the test's participants:

$$InQ = \frac{8 + 7 + 9 + 4 + 8}{5} = 7.2$$

As a reference, a score higher than 7 means you are now in an Inspirable phase of your life. If your result is around 5 or 6, you are in the transition zone, meaning you could be on the way to becoming inspirable, or the opposite and on the demotivation track to be un-inspirable. A typical person in an un-inspirable stage will score 4 or lower.

Chapter Insights

The Inspirable Quotient is a tool to guide you in your journey to become an inspirable person, and this is the sole reason I created it. I recommend taking the test every 3 to 6 months to check on your progress, but this is not essential. If you think you are making significant progress, keep going.

- The InQ test covers the five aspects of the Inspirable Way© model, so when you become familiar with it, you will see the benefits of measuring it immediately.
- I recommend first reflecting on your general InQ results and then reviewing if there is any specific area you should put your focus on.
- Keep your InQ test results or your InQ radar chart visible to increase your level of awareness of your development areas.

Chapter 5 - Becoming Inspirational

Learn the benefits and difficulties of the Inspirational phase

Your InQ can predict if you are becoming un-inspirable

Relate to the benefits of being close to good leaders

We were born inspirable, but as we grow through life, we lose some of our inspirable abilities. Our experiences with other people may influence how we see the world and increase our resistance to bonding with others, especially younger people.

I guess this happens because of the stereotypes created by society about other generations: the selfish Baby Boomers[17], cynical Generation X people[18], demanding Millennials[19], or the

---

[17] The Baby Boom refers to the increase of the birth rate that happened after World War II. Baby Boomers were born between 1946 and 1964.

[18] Gen X (born 1965-1980) is called so because when they became adults, they refused to be defined by the Baby Boomers, reflected the counterculture of a rebellious generation, distrustful of the establishment, and keen to find their own voice.

[19] The reason this group is called Millennials (born 1980-1996) is because they became adults and joined the workplace around the new millennium.

hyper-connected Generation Z[20]. This might also occur because connecting with people who have a fresh mindset usually requires some change in our own.

As you can see in Figure 3, the growth of this resistance to connect could be an indicator that you are on the journey to become un-inspirable. Eliminating this resistance is the mission of the Inspirable approach.

The first part of the journey starts when we are born, and it stretches until our first years in the workforce. When we join organizations, we are still sponges, absorbing all the surrounding knowledge. The Inspirable Quotient of a person in this stage is around 7 or 8. It is a stage marked by the excitement from the professional and the personal perspectives, as we become financially and emotionally independent from our parents and create inter-dependent relationships with our new circle.

We move to the second stage usually when we grow into management, taking over senior roles, specialist positions or become entrepreneurs. Now we are responsible for people's motivation; we need to become inspirational. There is an interesting phenomenon here. In the beginning of the inspirational stage, the need to provide better support to our teams motivates us to increase our knowledge in certain technical subjects but also managerial ones, such as managing performance, boosting motivation, and increasing team cohesion. This makes us grow, but it has a downside: We stop thinking about which areas are a priority for our own selfish development.

---

[20] This group was born after 1997, some of whom are now starting to join the workforce.

Figure 3: The Consciously Inspirable Journey

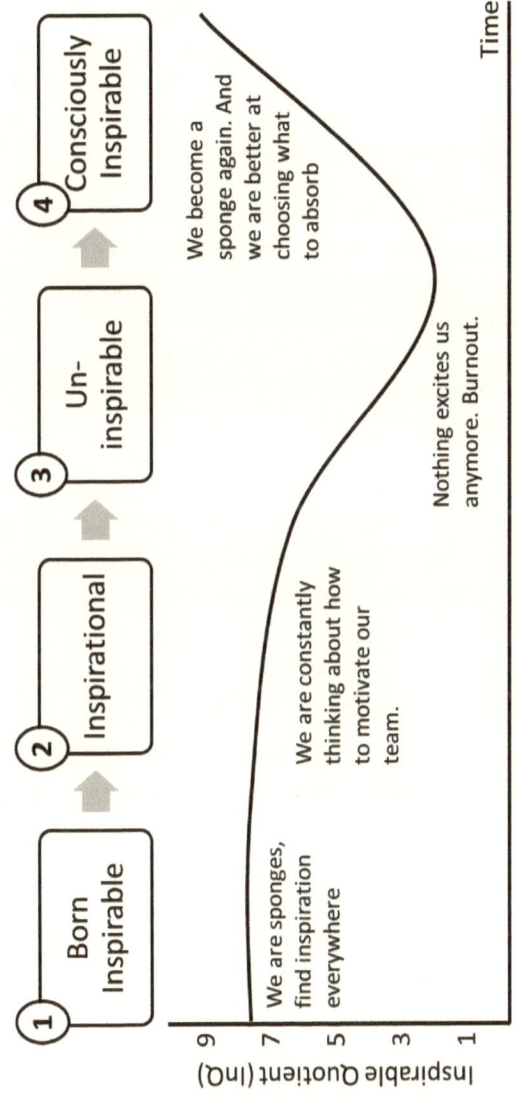

To make things worse, after you attain a certain level of proficiency in your managerial skills, your development comes to a halt, because *you have lost that drive and the habit of constant learning, and you have substituted it with the habit of problem-solving and firefighting.* Often, this situation is replicated in your personal life, as well. The Inspirable Quotient of the individual in this stage is between 5 and 6. The score itself is not bad, but the trend downward is.

After a while, we get tired and we become un-inspirable. Nothing amazes us. This causes the main disconnect between older and younger generations, and the separation from anyone who has ideas too different from ours. This is not exclusive to management; it is also frequent in specialists or technicians who become senior experts in their field. People in this stage have an InQ lower than 5.

The good news is we can go back to inspirable and embrace our differences again. Then we'll be working as equals with people 20 years younger or older than ourselves, behaving like sponges once more. The InQ of a person in this situation is usually 8 or 9, even higher than in the first stage because this time, *becoming inspirable is a conscious decision.*

Being inspirational is a good thing, but read the fine print

I have already told you about my first stage, when I was born inspirable. In this chapter, I'll share with you the experiences that made me inspirational, and in the next chapter, how I became un-inspirable.

Let's go back and talk about my experience at AES Corporation the energy multinational, as this was the one that revealed to me the value of inspiring my team and connecting multiple generations.

In 2003, a new marketing research department was created, and I was promoted to lead it. It was an exciting time because I was fortunate enough to choose my team of eight people from the talent already working within the company. The team I built was made up of enthusiastic women and men from different backgrounds. We welcomed colleagues from marketing, IT, and customer care. Some were 10 years younger than me, some 15 years older. This was definitely an exciting start to my first management experience. Until this moment, I had been inspirable during my whole professional career. Now I was taking a gigantic leap: I needed to become inspirational. My job was to boost the motivation and creativity of my team.

Everything was new for me, including my boss, who had just joined the company to lead the commercial business unit.

My new boss comes from the military

When I met Miguel, I had my doubts because he had a military background and I have never worked with someone from the armed forces before. I could imagine him yelling at me to do push-ups: "Drop and give me 20!" I, in my ignorance, swore I would never use military methods to lead my team.

I have to say that I was really fortunate to have him as the person who showed me how to be inspirational. My preconceived notion of what my new boss would be like was wrong, and I was never even politely asked to do a push-up. Miguel did bring a way to work that increased our efficiency tenfold, focusing less on company politics and more on boosting team engagement and customer satisfaction.

Most of the things he inspired me to do as a leader are almost common sense, but the most important thing to him was to make a real change. He believed it with his heart and positioned himself as a role model for every one of us. He showed by example how to:

- Set inspirational, attainable objectives.
- Stay super focused on the morale of the team.
- Adapt the communication style to embrace the diversity of the team.

Which was the key to connecting everyone on the team? I would say it was a special performance management approach. In any traditional organization, everyone on the team had SMART[21] objectives. However, we were very clear that people could bring a lot more value than just achieving these objectives. We were always discussing what intangible value every member was bringing to the team: some brought energy, others brought stability; some were innovators, several others were implementers.

We showed our commitment to every person, recognizing their value and supporting them when, for any reason, they didn't perform according to expectations. We acknowledged everyone was in a distinct moment of their lives; some were single, others were parents, few were close to retirement, and we could not ask for the same level of dedication.

We fired no one, and this created a psychological safety that encouraged everyone to speak up and bring new ideas. It was a hierarchical organization, but when we discussed business challenges, we behaved as equals.

---

[21] SMART performance objectives have to be: Specific, Measurable, Attainable, Relevant and Time-bound.

That dedication showed in the team's loyalty. We worked together for three years in a team of 81 people; nobody left the company.

I learned so much from Miguel about how to inspire others. I continued to use what I had discovered as I took on other management positions and went to work for other companies.

Taking an HR Director position in Tehran

In 2008, the political and economic situation in Venezuela was getting worse than it had been in several years. My wife and I explored options for international assignments and we agreed that whoever got the first option, the other would leave their job and follow.

I received an offer to work as HR director for a multinational company in Iran. The challenge was enormous from the cultural perspective, as well as from the business perspective. I talked to my wife, and we accepted the challenge. One month later, we were moving to Tehran.

Financially, this move was a very positive one, and it came with a lot of perks: I had an enormous apartment in the best place in town, a car and a driver, and I traveled business class all the time. If I told you I did not enjoy this, I would be lying. Later on, I think these were some of the stupid reasons that kept me in the company longer than I should have been.

The experience was exciting and stressful from every perspective. As an HR director, I had to boost the morale of a demotivated workforce that had been through frequent management changes. I had to work on a development plan for the employees in a country with few options for growth. Also,

I needed to make sure that we complied with every legal regulation, including, of course, those inspired by Islam, such as the dress and conduct codes.

There was a tremendous challenge: This was not a multigenerational environment, as most team members were in their 30s, and very few were near their 50s. You could think it was a homogeneous workplace from the generational perspective, but no, those who were 30 thought of the people who were close to 50 as old people, and vice versa, the people in their 50s perceived the younger ones as babies. The good news was that one guy was coming to town to bring this team together.

My Latino Boss in Iran

After three months in Iran, the company appointed a new boss. Jorge was the new general manager of the organization in Iran. He was also from Latin America, which helped me a lot as we got along pretty well. For the second time in my life, I had a supervisor that led by example and was not scared of being transparent.

In the beginning, it was difficult for me to get used to Jorge's straightforwardness. I felt he was even rude most of the time. But then, with time, I appreciated this guy as being honest. He would not say things that would make you happy if they weren't the right things to say. So, you knew whatever he said was exactly how he felt, and it was the truth.

Jorge was focused on speed, and I was not good at making quick decisions. I avoided taking risks, and I spent too much time ruminating about important business choices. His usual words were, "Do it!" If we weren't sure of something, he would say,

"So do it! Nobody is going to die. We are not doing heart surgery, so if something goes wrong, we'll fix it, and that's it." That way of thinking, and Jorge's support, made me a lot quicker when deciding and I was more willing to try new things. This new skill definitely paid off in future roles.

From Jorge I learned many things. The ones that have been most helpful were:

- Be straightforward. This will save you time and pain in the future. If you can be kind while doing it, great, but that's a plus.
- Make decisions quickly. If you think you are quick, be quicker. Stop ruminating.
- Speak up.
- You can be tough and demanding with people, as long as you are supportive.
- Everyone is important, regardless of age, gender, race, sexual orientation, or country of origin.

The most important thing that Jorge inspired me to do was *to be available to the people*. Every time I needed him, he made himself available as a boss, as a coach, or just to bounce off some ideas. If you think about it, it doesn't matter if you are a democratic or autocratic leader. If you are not available, you are not leading. I think this principle also applies if you want to be inspirable: You need to be available, you need to be there for others.

Jorge had high expectations, but he made sure the team had the tools to succeed.

We made tremendous changes to the business and improved the conditions of the staff in Iran. As much as I enjoyed working at this company, after two years, it was time to move on. It makes me proud to say that my replacement was the first woman (and

Iranian) to become the Human Resources director of the subsidiary.

This journey was so exciting for me that when it was time for me to move to Spain, I cried during my farewell in front of 150 people. Little did I know that my relocation to Spain was going to begin an un-inspirable journey.

Be In

Have you been inspirational?
Write three behaviors you remember from that time.

_____

_____

_____

_____

_____

_____

_____

Chapter Insights

We are born inspirable, and we usually stay that way until we join the workplace. Then our responsibilities grow, we become managers or specialists, and our roles demand we become inspirational, motivating others.

- Being inspirational boosts our development in the beginning as we want to learn more to provide better support for our teams.
- But it also makes us lose the direction of our own development. This, in time, makes us un-inspirable.

Chapter 6 - Becoming Un-inspirable

Are you in your current situation for the wrong reasons?

Have you weighed the pros and cons of your decision?

Have you calculated the cost of not changing?

Madrid is the joyful and exciting capital of Spain. Visitors and residents alike enjoy the beautifully landscaped parks like El Retiro or El Capricho, and the stylish boulevards of Calle Serrano. It is world-renowned for its European art displayed in museums like El Prado, Thyssen-Bornemisza, or Reina Sofia, as well as its celebrated restaurants with delectable cuisine. It also has a variety of neighborhoods and cultural centers and is filled with charming family-run bars where you meet friends for drinks after work or shopping on a Saturday afternoon.

What attracted me the most to this city was the welcoming feeling of belonging. Many foreigners who visit decide to stay here, and Madrid is open to that. Spain has many amazing cities and small towns to settle in, such as Barcelona, San Sebastian, Valencia, and Seville. Each of them has different advantages (weather, beaches, mountains) but most people in Spain will agree with me when I say that Madrid is the most heterogeneous

Spanish city, so much so that there is a saying, "No one in Madrid is *from* Madrid!" People here are from different parts of Spain and the rest of the world, with the biggest groups coming from other countries of the European Union, Latin-America, north Africa, and China.

It is an especially welcoming place for Spanish-speaking Latin Americans like me. I fell in love with the people of Madrid immediately.

But the company was a different story

I started as HR director for Spain and Portugal for a company in January 2010, and it thrilled me to be there. I also loved the people in the company; it was as welcoming and diverse as Madrid itself, with a highly skilled group of people.

The working environment was a completely different story, and not a positive one. When I was working with Miguel in Venezuela or with Jorge in Iran, I felt we wanted to make important changes for a better future. I did not get this feeling from the team in Spain where many team members felt demotivated, insecure, and disengaged. Later on, I found the root cause of this in the conduct of some leadership team members, who were more concerned with perks, salaries, and climbing the ladder than really improving and making long-lasting changes.

From the beginning, it didn't feel right, but I wanted to belong and to be accepted, so I imitated their behavior. I went against my instincts and neglected to bring my leadership style to the table. It doesn't matter what I thought of the leadership team; I was responsible for my actions, no matter the influences around me.

The plight of the lemming

Everything went downhill once I started following the crowd like the lemmings that jump off of cliffs in groups because of their migratory behavior[22]. I lost my passion for the job and spent much of my workday glancing at the clock, focused more on when it was time to go home. Conversations about the business seemed shallow, and every meeting seemed endless for me. I lost my ability or even desire to inspire others, and I definitely was no longer inspirable.

I dare to say that for some of us, those meetings were just about surviving, and for others it was just a game. There was no genuine sense of achievement or purpose for any, and no need for taking risks. Everyone I worked with was pretty much the same age as me — from the same generation — and there was no exchanging of ideas or expectations of getting out of our comfort zones. My most common behaviors included:

- Talking about things I wanted to buy that I did not need.
- Talking about trips we should take to escape our lives.
- Pretending to be someone I was not: an aggressive corporate animal. And I was terrible at it.
- Gossiping about other people: about the job they had and stuff they owned.

The world was changing around me, and I was burning years off my life in a meeting room. Meanwhile, more and more important businesses were joining the online world, and I was stuck in a company that was against engaging in social networks. Other companies were exploring different ways of

---

[22]The Plight of the Lemming serves as a metaphor of someone who blindly follows a crowd toward catastrophe. Encyclopaedia Britannica "Do Lemmings Really Commit Mass Suicide?"
https://www.britannica.com/story/do-lemmings-really-commit-mass-suicide

communicating that saved travel time and were more responsible with the environment, but my company blocked Skype from every computer. Exciting ventures were growing such as Uber, Airbnb, and Fiverr; we were still sitting around the campfire trying to figure out how to invent the wheel.

The triggers for resignation

After two years in Spain, I got to work with the most un-inspiring boss I ever had. He was incredibly difficult to work for, and because of him, I considered leaving the company. I've been fortunate to have many bosses in my career who were decent people. During the 20 years of my corporate career, I think I had around 15 supervisors who were easy to get along with and many inspired me along my journey, so this one arrived at the exact moment in my life to trigger the perfect storm.

Although I was more convinced every day about quitting, my wife was very resistant to the idea of my resignation because she had given up her job before we moved from Venezuela. She was worried about our financial safety if I quit because she didn't have a job in Madrid.

When I was working corporate in Madrid, we enjoyed the business perks. I felt like I deserved them and it was nice to have a spacious apartment. Somehow, we lost sight of what was really important in our lives. We were unconsciously or consciously connected to money, things, and perks as well as the fear of losing them. This thinking had a hold on me and kept me at the job a couple of years longer than it should have. I don't feel proud of that because it's so stupid. I lived in a state of fear and I felt old at 37; more than 10 years later, I still feel so much younger than I did then.

My wife and I went then on a trip to Cambodia that cleared our minds. I know it sounds like a cliché, but it was truly an awakening for us. This breathtaking country reminded us of the simple pleasures in life. We had to live without the luxury of fancy lodgings. The surrounding beauty, the kind people, and being with each other was everything we needed.

On the way back, we stopped for a few days in Bangkok, and on the afternoon of the second day, we found ourselves at a very simple restaurant next to the Chao Phraya River. I remember looking around at the scenery and feeling so peaceful as we enjoyed our bowls of white rice and bottled beer. My wife smiled at me with a knowing look and said, "Go ahead, quit."

The first day I went back to work in Madrid, I went straight to the office of my boss to hand him the letter of resignation. We had a very honest conversation about how difficult we were making each other's lives and we ended with a friendly agreement about my leaving. I just needed to find a person to replace me and do a proper handover.

It took seven months to find my replacement, and the interesting thing is that I enjoyed those months with the same intensity as when I worked in inspiring environments. I finally spoke up and others listened. I attended only the meetings that were productive, and I dedicated my time listening to employees rather than being busy with PowerPoints. I was in the same place with the same boss and co-workers; I was the same person and everything was the same as before. The fact that I was resigning took all the pressure off of me and I was no longer fearful. I was the happiest I'd been in a long time during those seven months.

This temporary joy did not cause any regrets about my decision to leave because I was sure I wanted to experience the transformation that was happening in the professional world in an environment more open to it. This change in my mood made a tremendous difference because it made me understand that my interpretation of the situation and, most importantly, my self-isolation from inspirational people were the major causes of becoming un-inspirable.

My handover process was so positive, the CEO approved a "good leaver" exit with special conditions to show appreciation for my performance. It was a great way to close this chapter in my life.

On my last day, after many individual farewells, I said goodbye to everyone with hugs and tears of happiness. Alfonso, from the regional HR team, was very kind to accompany me out of the building. It was a happy coincidence that he was in the group who greeted me when I arrived in Spain almost three years before.

I had given my car back to the company, so I took the metro to our new home. We were not living in the company's rented apartment anymore as we had bought a new one in a beautiful area of Madrid that we loved.

We had mixed feelings at the beginning of this new era: fear and excitement, but overall, we felt free. This is ours! This is our stuff! The real us is here!

Then we started the most exciting journey of our lives.

Be In

Have you ever suffered burnout? Which were your symptoms? Did you become less sociable when this happened?

_____

_____

_____

_____

_____

_____

_____

_____

Chapter Insights

In retrospect I can see four chief causes that took me from being an inspirational leader to an un-inspirable person:

1. Ego. Becoming inspirational, or at least thinking that you are, comes with a dangerous condition: If you are not careful, your ego gets bigger than your actual worth. Big egos are enormous obstacles to development because why would you need to develop if you're already so great?

2. A job without an interesting challenge. After having so much freedom in my jobs in Venezuela and Iran, the organization I joined in Spain was about "going back to basics." I'm not saying that is wrong, just that I was not right for the task. If you recruit people that embrace risk-taking and out-of-the-box thinking, it is difficult to tell

them that their major challenge will be to bring the business back to basics.

3. Fear of not belonging. This made me embrace behaviors that were against my values and my leadership style. This made it very painful to go to work every day. Thinking back, I realize that the lack of a solid, personal network in Madrid also fueled this fear. Expat life is a bit lonely until you settle down.

4. Self-isolating from inspirational people. There were interesting people on the team, and some of them are still my good friends. However, I was focusing only on the negatives. If I were inspirable in the same environment, I could have had a different experience. Would it have ended with my resignation in the end? Yes, but with a more productive journey.

PART II - CONSCIOUSLY INSPIRABLE

Chapter 7 - The Inspirable Way©

How are longevity and technology affecting your workplace?

Which are the three most important assets to have in this new era?

How can you become inspirable?

Adult development is a fairly recent concept. During the 20th century, with the growth of the big corporations and the concept of employment for life, human lives became divided into three periods[23]:

1.   Formal education, from school to college

2.   Working years

3.   Retirement

---

[23] Although during the 20th century employee engagement was very important, as people were employed for life, they accepted stability in exchange for not necessarily staying inspirable their whole careers, so no investments were made from neither the employer nor employee to achieve this.

I will describe the mood that dominated during these three stages as it relates to the first three of four steps of the Consciously Inspirable journey.

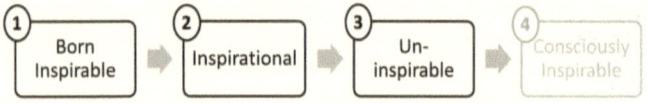

Figure 4: Short version of the Consciously Inspirable Journey

In the first part of life, from formal education to your first years of work, the most common description is that you are enjoying the inertia of being born inspirable. It is easy for you to be impressed by the surrounding people, and you will usually imitate the behavior you believe will be more productive for you.

Moving into the second stage of your working life, usually when you get to a managerial position with more responsibilities that include taking care of a team or you become an experienced specialist, your focus shifts to becoming inspirational. Your primary goal will be to motivate your team or junior people and lead by example. This stage can be as exciting as the first one, but beware, this could also cause that you don't take enough care of your own development.

It is common that after many years of trying to keep your team engaged and coping in parallel with all the business and workplace challenges, many people get what is called burnout syndrome.

Burnout is a state of emotional, physical, and mental exhaustion caused by excessive and prolonged stress. It occurs when you feel overwhelmed, emotionally drained, and unable to meet constant demands[24].

I was familiar with the concept after years suffering with it. It is just recently that I realized the major consequence of burnout is becoming un-inspirable, the third stage of the journey.

Why is burnout more important now than 50 years ago?

When you had a job for life, your expectation was that it could cover your basic needs and, in the best-case scenario, some social mobility to a higher status. It was not expected that the job itself had to be a source of self-realization. Nowadays, we have financial and developmental demands for our jobs, as well as the need for flexibility. The job has to be aligned with our purpose and our values, and when this is not fulfilled, we try to switch jobs. The same happens on the employer's side: They demand that the function they hired you for gets done, but also demand a positive attitude, pro-activeness, and empathy. When this does not happen, they want another person in your place.

So, if in the past you studied accounting, you retired as an accountant, and the same happened with every other career. Now, when the person is burnt out, they usually leave the company (voluntarily or not). As we live longer, we work more years, which means we are having multiple professional cycles.

---

[24] Melinda Smith, M.A., Jeanne Segal, Ph.D., and Lawrence Robinson. "Burnout Prevention and Treatment." November 2021.
https://www.helpguide.org/articles/stress/burnout-prevention-and-recovery.htm#:~:text=Burnout%20is%20a%20state%20of,unable%20to%20meet%20constant%20demands

This raises the importance of becoming inspirable again after a burnout.

Before I talk more about this subject, I want to share with you some challenges that are influencing the dynamics in the workplace.

Longevity increases

Longevity has exploded during the past few decades. The average life expectancy worldwide in the year 1950 was 50 years, jumping to 64 years in 1990 and now a whooping 73 years in 2019. Japan is in first place with a life expectancy of 85 years, followed closely by South Korea, many European countries, Canada, and Australia[25].

With longevity increase, pension systems are under stress in almost every country, and this has resulted in the need to work for more years. By 2020, the normal retirement age of men has increased in 20 out of 38 OECD countries[26].

This is not just a financial challenge. From the individual perspective, this requires a complete redefinition of life priorities.

We had a recipe for a fulfilling a 70-year life that was created in the 20th century: Get educated, work, retire. That was a good

---

[25] Max Roser, Esteban Ortiz-Ospina and Hannah Ritchie. "Life Expectancy." *Our World in Data.* 2013. https://ourworldindata.org/life-expectancy

[26] Organisation for Economic Cooperation and Development. *Pensions at a Glance 2021: OECD and G20 Indicators.*
https://www.oecd-ilibrary.org/sites/ca401ebd-
en/1/3/3/6/index.html?itemId=/content/publication/ca401ebd-
en&_csp_=9d37797bd84847326841f27f588be463&itemIGO=oecd&itemCon
tentType=book

formula for an average working life of 30-35 years[27], but what happens if we live 100-year lives and need to work for 50 or 60 years?

Lynda Gratton and Andrew J. Scott[28] address this dilemma in their book *The 100-Year Life*. Their proposal states we should flee from the three-stage life to one of multiple stages. To do this, you must acquire three types of intangible assets: productive, vital, and transformational.

Productive assets are those that help individuals become valuable and therefore boost their income. Most productive assets are very tangible, like properties or financial investments, but Gratton and Scott put their focus on the intangible part: growing knowledge and skills. An example of this could be learning a second language, improving your managerial skills, or understanding how to code.

Vitality assets are those practices that bring physical and mental health. This includes having friends and positive family relationships, healthy eating habits, working out regularly, and using stress management practices like mindfulness and meditation.

Transformation assets are of a different order. In a longer life, individuals will have to go through more stages and transitions. Three transformational assets are key for this journey, beginning with attaining self-knowledge through an honest evaluation of yourself. Who do you want to become in the

---

[27] "Duration of working life – statistics." *Statistics Explained.* July 1, 2022. https://ec.europa.eu/eurostat/statistics-explained/index.php?title=Duration_of_working_life_-_statistics#:~:text=In%202020%2C%20the%20estimated%20expected,women%20it%20was%2033.2%20years

[28] Lynda Gratton and Andrew Scott. *The 100-Year Life: Living and Working in an Age of Longevity.* (New York: Bloomsbury Business, 2016.)

future? Second, you'll need to create diverse networks of people drawn from different social circles, geographies, and generations. Third, there needs to be an openness to new experiences and ideas, as well as a willingness to experiment with new behaviors.

The Inspirable Way© is a method designed to grow these three kinds of assets to enjoy longevity as the blessing it should be. As you will see, these assets are also vital for our present to comfortably face the challenges that technological disruptions are bringing to our organization, our professional careers, and our lives.

Be In

Which are the main intangible assets you need to start developing right away: productive, vitality or transformational?

_____

_____

_____

_____

_____

_____

_____

Technological change and the future of professions

Along with the increase in longevity, technological progress has become one of the main shapers of professions and workplaces.

Most times automation and artificial intelligence have become great complements to human work, helping people go faster, further, and cheaper. We always took for granted that this had to be the role of technology. Despite many experts saying that it could be a substitute for human labor, we disregarded it as another attempt by the media to create panic. Even when we considered the possibility, we never thought they were talking about our job. Technology was meant to take care of simple tasks so that humans could handle the complex ones. This was the main reason for carrying a big brain on our shoulders for thousands of years, wasn't it?

However, I started observing that the opposite was happening. A few years ago, I was on a business trip to London. As I was going through British customs, I realized every part of the process was completely automatic now. I scanned my passport at the gate, and I guess a computer analyzed my records to verify that I was not a terrorist or a person who intended to do the wrong kind of business in the UK. A few seconds later, the gate opened the doors of the country and let me in, with no one touching or stamping my passport's now useless pages.

At first, I was amazed by what had happened, but later on during the day I thought, what were the customs employees doing while all this was happening? They were calling the people in the queue and telling them to which gate they should go. I have many other examples where computers are doing the complex tasks and humans doing the simple ones.

I don't dare to predict the future of work, as many prophets have failed foretelling the end of work during the first, second, and third industrial revolutions[29] and somehow, we still created

---

[29] Klaus Schwab. "The Fourth Industrial Revolution: what it means, how to respond." *World Economic Forum.* January 14, 2016.

more jobs and more value to society. But father and son Richard and Daniel Susskind took the risk and projected two scenarios:

❝❝

"The first is reassuringly familiar to most professionals— it is simply a more efficient version of what we have today. In this future, professionals of different types use technology, but essentially to streamline and optimize their traditional ways of working. In the language of economists, technologies complement them in these activities. The second future is a different proposition. Here, increasingly capable systems and machines, either operating alone or designed and operated by people who look quite unlike doctors and lawyers, teachers and accountants, and others, gradually take on more of the tasks that we associate with those traditional professionals. New technologies instead, in the words of economists, substitute for professionals in these activities."[30]

The authors don't blame it only on technological progress. They argue that our current professions are antiquated and no longer sustainable. In a world where collaboration is a must, we cannot afford to have so many people behaving as gatekeepers in organizations, having partial views and solutions to problems

---

https://www.weforum.org/agenda/2016/01/the-fourth-industrial-revolution-what-it-means-and-how-to-respond/

[30] Susskind, Richard, and Daniel Susskind. *The Future of the Professions: How Technology Will Transform the Work of Human Experts.* (Oxford: Oxford University Press, 2015.

that are becoming more complex and require multidisciplinary approaches.

Adult development became fundamental

The increase in longevity, the constant technological changes, and its impact on business models required individuals to look for ways to develop themselves.

Technical training like workshops, seminars, and graduate studies became abundant. Alternatives like mentoring, executive coaching, and change management also became popular to train soft skills such as leadership, adaptability, and collaboration.

Interestingly enough, this second part of *development actions that involved mindset change was quite a lonely journey* for those who were taking it. You were, in the best cases, working around your obstacles with your coach, your mentor, or your boss, but most of the time on your own.

The problem with this structure is twofold. First, it takes a lot of time for change to happen, and second, it requires a lot of willpower (coaches call it "commitment") not to quit. It is not a joyful process but painful.

And if you fail, it is your fault.

As the need to collaboration increases and we go deeper into the 21st century, we understand that collaboration is not only a means to an end but a big option to boost adult development. And yet, most development processes nowadays follow the same structure as 40 years ago.

The need for a new development model

Starting my corporate life in 1995 and performing roles as human resources director, executive coach, and mentor, I have witnessed the stagnation of these approaches. After observing so many individuals and teams failing to improve, I came up with some ideas of my own.

What was most common in the successful change processes I witnessed? Those who wanted to grow had a source of inspiration. They don't want just to achieve something; they want to become a better person.

However, inspiration is volatile, so you cannot rely on one shot of inspiration to push you all the way. You need constant inspiration, from many sources and living examples, walking around you every day. It means we need to embed the greatest skill of all. We need to become inspirable.

We need to become inspirable

Inspirable is the capacity to make yourself more permeable to the positive behaviors of those with who you connect. Remember, it is about bonding, but you don't need to create bonds with Simon Sinek or Brené Brown to become inspirable. This is about connecting with people in or near your personal network. Seeing neighbors, colleagues, and acquaintances facing many challenges to develop further is what makes you jump off the couch and try to imitate them. That makes you inspirable because you have seen normal people transform themselves.

How can you become inspirable? *The Inspirable Way©* is a sequence that will get you there.

Figure 5: The Inspirable Way

- **Inspirable Self** is about exploring the kind of change you want in your life.
- You will learn to rely on your **Inspirable Tribe** to become the person you want to be.
- The **Inspirable Context** step helps you change your context in the workplace or home to make it fit your aspirations.
- When you are ready to define actions for your tribe's development, you'll need **Inspirable Moves**.

- During this cycle, you will accumulate **Inspirable Gains**, so you will appreciate your progress, not against your ideals or goals, but compared to who you were before.

You will become permeable to your environment and open to connect with different people, whether they're younger, older, smarter, wiser, or just interesting. This approach will not drain your willpower, and the feeling of joy will grow with every step that you take.

You will benefit from this approach regardless of any stage you are in according to your InQ. It will be a true-life savior if you are in the un-inspirable stage; at least it was for me, as I will share in the next chapter. I'm sure that you will relate to what happened to me, and then how I started my move back to becoming Consciously Inspirable, following without knowing some of the steps of the model I just introduced you to.

Be In

Describe the last time you had a learning experience that changed the way you do things? Were you on your own or with other participants? How did the other participants contribute to your transformation?

_____

_____

_____

_____

_____

_____

_____

_____

Chapter Insights

Longevity has soared during the past five decades. For financial and relationships reasons, we might benefit from working more years.

- To do this, we need to develop productivity, vitality, and transformational assets.
- In a longer working life, you will be burnt out several times and become un-inspirable many times, as well.

The Inspirable Way© is the approach to get you out of those slumps quicker and avoid some pitfalls so that you live a healthy life, constantly growing personally and professionally.

Chapter 8 - Step 1: The Inspirable Self

Which are your three priorities for improvement?

How can you make them exciting instead of daunting?

Start focusing on the process and the outcome will come.

The first step out of the un-inspirable stage toward an inspirable way of life is to explore the areas of your life that you need to develop to have a more fulfilling time while you walk this earth.

I will intentionally talk about exploration and self-discovery in this book. Despite what many rigid personal growth approaches say, this one is based on the idea that you need flexibility to develop. Your life is always changing, making it unreasonable to stick to fixed objectives for longer than you should. You will not read the words "define" or "determine" very often here, as those words belong to more strict frameworks.

Society is always pushing us to make decisions, even when we don't have to. From a young age, people around you want to know when you're going to college, what you are going to major in, when you're going to get married, when you're going to have children, and if you've started your retirement fund. As a father, I continuously hear other parents ask their children if they want to be this or that. I've always wondered if they really need to make up their minds when they are only 7 years old or 17 years old, or even 37 years old.

Don't get me wrong, I don't think you should be paralyzed most of your life, stagnant and unwilling to make any determinations whatsoever, but I think life is too long and changing so frequently that even our determinations should be reviewed now and then.

Mark Manson, the author of the bestseller *The Subtle Art of Not Giving a F*ck*, has a brilliant thought that illustrates this point:

"

"Every step of the way I was wrong. About everything. Throughout my life, I've been flat-out wrong about myself, others, society, culture, the world, the universe — everything. And I hope that will continue to be the case for the rest of my life. Just as Present Mark can look back on Past Mark's every flaw and mistake, one day Future Mark will look back on Present Mark's assumptions [...] and notice similar flaws. And that will be a good thing. Because that will mean I have grown."[31]

---

[31] Mark Manson. *The Subtle Art of Not Giving a F*ck: A Counterintuitive Approach to Living a Good Life*. (New York, NY: Harper, 2016.)

This chapter is about exploring who you want to be. By exploring instead of deciding, you will have more freedom to take action and adapt to varying desires; and you will suffer less anxiety because you are not deciding for the rest of your lifetime. This is the reason this part of the journey is about investigating who you want to be. You'll search for new ideas, seek answers, and inquire about interesting possibilities. Hence, exploration is part of the solution.

Improving life areas

The first step as you explore who you want to be is to choose three main areas of your life that you would like to improve. It could be areas where you feel you are not doing well or areas where you are doing fine but you want to thrive.

Sometimes I prefer to focus on areas where I am doing fine but I want to do way better. This is the Good to Great approach.[32] However, when I was un-inspirable, the three areas that I picked were the ones I was completely unsatisfied with: taking part in interesting projects, incorporating healthier habits, and leading a joyful life.

When doing this, I want to invite you to think about the long term. Longevity is a challenge, so remember the three main assets we have to develop to live a great 100-year life: Productivity, Vitality, and Transformation. You can check them again in Chapter 7 if you need to.

---

[32] In personal development the most common approach has been to focus on the weak areas and develop those, but there are other approaches that say focus on your strengths and develop those even further. There are interesting classics supporting the second option: 1. Buckingham, Coffman, and Harter, *First, Break All the Rules*. And 2. Collins, *Good to Great*.

To make your job easier, I have prepared a list of the categories that I hear about most often in my growth conversations with entrepreneurs, professionals, students, business leaders and homemakers:

Health & well-being	Professional	Relationships
Leadership	Impact	Family
Spirituality	Happiness	Sustainability
Learning	Financial	Organizational
Employability	Entrepreneurship	Retirement
Emotional intelligence	Mindfulness	Technology

Table 2 Development areas

Once you have determined your three picks, it is advisable to describe what each of the three means for you. This will make it easier for you to understand what you want to achieve. Let me explain the three evolution areas that I explored when I started my journey to become inspirable:

1. **Taking part in interesting projects.** I wanted to be involved in interesting professional and personal endeavors with people I admire and needed to make a difference in society. I believe technology is now an inseparable piece of human well-being improvement, so the projects I join should have a human behavior understanding element and a technological one.

2. **Incorporating healthier habits.** Having a powerful body with hardly any limitations to move, run, and stretch will be an excellent vehicle for my aging. I wanted to have a healthy, peaceful mind that helps me embrace life's challenges with excitement rather than anxiety.

3. **Leading a joyful life.** I didn't want to go through life as the "grumpy guy." I yearn to have optimistic thoughts that make me smile frequently. I intend to have a thinking mind, but not a worried one. I have had a fortunate life, so I chose to behave accordingly.

To summarize, *the inspirable person who I wanted to become was a healthier, joyful person, and involved in interesting projects*. To be honest, if you create a statement like this, it is more than enough, but for the sake of having a better taste of that future self, I recommend elaborating further. Which would be the most common behaviors you would do when you become inspirable?

New behaviors

Keep in mind these behaviors are only a guide for your development. It is not an action plan that you should start doing tomorrow. The only purpose of writing them down is to create a better understanding of the inspirable person you want to explore. I also want to warn you don't start executing actions on your own. If you try to tackle this solo, without your Inspirable Tribe, you might end up getting the same result you got in the past: giving up. My suggestion is to wait a few chapters and you will understand why I am asking you to hold.

Going back to new behaviors, these were some things I imagined myself doing when I started becoming inspirable:

In the area of **interesting projects**, I thought about participating in professional initiatives that help accelerate workplace transformation. I also wanted to get involved in research projects with academic institutions and students. I knew working together with younger generations was what could keep me constantly developing.

About generating **healthy habits,** I imagined myself going regularly to the gym, eating healthier foods, reducing desserts and sodas, and cutting down on alcoholic beverages. I definitely longed to incorporate meditation into my life, which could help me be more present all the time. Last but not least, I wanted to sleep a minimum of 7 hours a day.

And regarding **a joyful life**, I saw myself engaging in joyful activities completely unrelated to work, like dancing lessons, bonsai growing, and spending more time with friends.

When thinking about the behaviors, I realized it was very easy to list the ones related to work and the interesting projects. The health part was also easy, as I had been thinking about it for a while, but the joy part was tough for me because living a joyful life had never been part of my priorities, so I could not imagine what people full of joy do to stay that way. The beauty of this approach is that nothing is definitive. Everything can be changed, so my perception of a joyful life started changing as soon as I intended to live one.

Now visualize

Many people use visualization to achieve great transformations. An athlete may picture himself training responsibly, taking care of his body so that he can take part in many events without injuries. A singer may envision herself practicing every day with her voice coach so that she can hit that high note in her final song for that concert. The CEO of a Fortune 500 company visualizes feeling confident while presenting a new product to the board.

You don't have to be runner Usain Bolt or artist Lady Gaga to have a transformation worth visualizing. You may want to look for a new job or begin a healthier eating habit. No matter what you want to improve, you can use visualization techniques to focus on success.

How does visualization help? Visualization is important because it is the only way you can reward yourself with the benefits in advance, knowing you will get there once you're successful. Your brain is always looking for immediate rewards to prioritize the actions you are going to take. Visualization helps you spark a neurotransmitter called dopamine. Because it feels good to see yourself with a strong habit of going to the gym every day or working joyfully on the book you want to write, you're more likely to get yourself into the action.

Visualization can motivate you, give you confidence, reduce your anxiety, and give you a "practice run."[33] Listing many details about what your future will be like will make it more tangible, more real. This technique helps you keep your journey in mind all the time and inspires you to keep going.

I asked myself, how will my life be like if my three areas of focus (interesting projects, healthy habits and joyful life) improve? Here are my answers:

- I will have more energy, be more productive, and I will need to work fewer hours.
- I will spend most of the time working on solutions for actual problems with less rumination.
- My self-confidence will start growing. As I get stronger, my posture improves and my joints come to be more flexible. The thoughts of aging will not go away (because it is a fact) but will not be a big concern to me as I will feel younger.
- I will be in contact with interesting people all over the world, gaining new skills and developing a more global

---

[33] Jayson DeMers. "13 Visualization Techniques to Help You Reach Your Goals". Lifehack. March 22, 2022.
https://www.lifehack.org/883519/visualization-techniques

worldview that will help me understand and relativize my local problems.

- The reduction of my anxiety levels will allow me to be fully present with my family, when at my work, and with my students.

When you go through the visualization process, you will actually feel the excitement of these things happening, releasing dopamine, which will give you the initial boost to kick off your journey.

Other techniques for visualization

There are many techniques for visualization, and each individual must find what works for them. The most popular one is simply using your imagination to create the scene. A good way to visualize is to sit comfortably with your eyes closed and breathe deeply. Then bring the situation to life in your mind and imagine success. For example, you could do some visualization daily, imagining yourself in your future life, walking, breathing, and feeling strong. Or you could envision family time and how it would feel to be relaxed while you enjoy them. Then you are more likely to stick to your workout schedule because you will feel what it's like to be healthier. You'll put that phone away at 8 p.m. in anticipation of a better rest.

Another technique is the dream board, which can be a daily reminder of the path you have taken. People usually cut out magazine pictures and write quotes that show their intentions manifested.

Whatever visualization tool you use, it will surely help you on your voyage as you explore who you want to be. Don't settle on any one answer or commit to what others think you should do. Give yourself lots of room to discover your true self.

Remember, visualizing only results can even derail you from accomplishing the transformation you want. Nir Eyal, an Israeli-born American best-selling author, lecturer, and investor[34] says that visualizing an outcome or goal—for example, I want to lose 5 kilograms—can create an emotion similar to already having accomplished it, so your brain will eliminate it from your priority list, making it very hard to achieve.

So, what is the best way to do it then?

Eyal talks about visualizing the process. You need to imagine the things that you are going to be doing to make it happen. Because the actions that you perform are the ones that are going to get you closer to the life you want, instead of visualizing losing 5 kilograms, visualize yourself eating healthier or drinking less booze.

My students might visualize the grade that they want to get, but most importantly, they should imagine themselves studying, enjoying the learning process, putting more focus on the different subjects, and reducing distractions.

Going back to my example, most of my visualizations are around processes. I visualize myself meditating daily, eating healthier, sleeping more, and contacting interesting people. Most of the time, results have followed.

Visualization is a very personal exercise, and being inspirable is about bonding, so how does an individual practice fit within a tribe-based approach? Well, defining who you want to be is

---

[34] Nir Eyal. "What You Need to Know When Visualizing Your Goals." January 27, 2020. https://www.nirandfar.com/visualizing/.

an individual decision. This is the only step of the cycle that I ask you to take on your own. However, every time I visualize my path, I also include in the visualization *who else can accompany me or inspire me in this journey*.

Be In

Write down the three main areas of your life where you want to do better to become an Inspirable Self. Write down in one paragraph or two of your visualization: How would your life be if you improve in these three areas?

_____

_____

_____

_____

_____

_____

_____

_____

Chapter Insights

Step 1 of the Inspirable Way© is to explore who you want to become and identify which three main areas you should develop to get closer to the person you would like to be.

If you compare this step with most of the personal development options available, you will find many similarities. However, there are key differences:

- Most of the other approaches help you achieve goals and this one helps you become a better person.
- Other development options depend on your strict commitment to achieving a goal and the Inspirable Way© takes for granted that your aim will change as you evolve, avoiding a fixed mindset from the start.
- Frequent visualization of how your life will look in the future if you improve acts as a powerful joy booster for your development journey. When visualizing your future, remember to focus on the process: What will you be doing to get you where you want to be? The results will come by themselves.

Chapter 9 - Finding Inspiration

Realize the value of who you are,

is as important as exploring who you want to be,

and as important as the tribes you belong to.

I was on cloud nine as I walked out of the company building for the last time, back straight, head held high. I had made a big decision and now I was in control of my life. I felt such immense relief. But that elation began to deflate.

I was still confident it was a solid decision because I needed fresh air, and staying with the company would have defeated that purpose. What did I want? Until then, I don't think I realized the impact of asking oneself that question. While the prospect of new adventures exhilarated me, it also scared me to death.

I don't want you to think I quit my job under a rain of confetti and balloons and lived happily ever after. No, this decision had costs. It was certainly worth it in the end, but first I had to go through unemployment and the reinventing of my self-identity.

I knew from my old, almost forgotten experiences as a coach that I needed to define an objective if I wanted to move on. And with that aim in mind, plan the actions to reach it and visualize all the benefits this could bring to me. This will provide the energy needed for my transformation journey.

The birth of the Inspirable Way

Soon enough, I realized something was wrong in this process. I was so confused that I could not work in this type of planning, nor was I in the mood to go back to the world of objectives, deadlines, and frustrations. I had recently taken the reigns of my life back, and I was not willing to give them up so easily. It was a tricky situation; I couldn't define where I wanted to go, but I was willing to start the exploration right away.

So, I did just that. I chose the three areas of improvement I mentioned in the previous chapter: interesting projects, healthy habits and joyful life, and I did a visualization of what my life would look like if these three areas improved. I could have chosen two or four areas, but those were the right ones for me then. This was the birth of Step 1 of the Inspirable Way©: The Inspirable Self.

Lost in the wilderness

The change was big, and I could not have foreseen most of the variables that were affected by my decision. I didn't have a job and was not sure where I was going next and what I was going to do. Everything within that first year was very tough. It wasn't the dream I expected. I felt like a stranded person, struggling to find his way through dense forests and undiscovered territory.

From a couple's perspective, it became difficult to support each other mentally and spiritually. My wife and I were partners in life and finances, but we no longer had a steady flow of income and that damaged our foundation. Life was better with fewer luxurious unnecessary items, and we have kept a simple life since then, but there was too much happening and too much uncertainty to handle.

This situation made me understand that turning un-inspirable can spread to other aspects of your life and hurt those you love the most.

My wife and I separated, so it was becoming really messy. I was struggling and feeling insecure, although I still believed in my decision. My wife and I had an underlying faith in each other, so during the storm, we worked to rebuild our marriage, and a few months later, we were again a team. As of today, we still are.

I was adapting. I had to find ways to change in order to survive. I had never been an entrepreneur. I've had a paycheck every month during the previous 16 years, so I didn't know how to make money on my own. Without a job, position, or company name behind me, I lost my self-confidence. My emotions went back and forth between the hopefulness of new possibilities and worrying about the future.

So, who was I now? I was not an HR director. I didn't belong to X Company or Y Company. I was just me. Sometimes walking away from the complexities of life will give you a raw understanding of your true identity. This was a turning point in the journey. The panorama looked brighter immediately after I hit rock bottom.

Getting my citizenship

Some important chips fell into place soon enough to bring some stability and get the excitement flowing. A few months after leaving the company, we gained Spanish citizenship. Now we were free to live and do business in any part of Spain and the European Union.

In terms of my life and the life of my family, it was a significant milestone. By the time I started writing this book, almost 6 million people from my home country Venezuela have migrated[35] because of an economic crisis completely mismanaged by the ruling regime. So, citizenship means having a new home and a new opportunity to dream. I will always be grateful to Spain and its people for adopting us. A year later, our daughter Sara was born in a free country. The future was looking brighter.

How my hobby helped me find my connection again

In parallel with the crisis I was going through personally, I enjoyed dedicating more hours to what was my then hobby: photography. It's interesting how it worked because after I left the company, I lost my desire to take photos of people. All I wanted to shoot were landscapes.

---

[35] "Venezuelan Migrant and Refugee Crisis." International Organization for Migration. January 2022.
https://www.iom.int/venezuelan-refugee-and-migrant-crisis

In retrospective, I think it was a kind of therapy. After working in HR and with people-related functions for so many years, I think I needed time away from the public.

During this transition period, my wife and I ventured to different countries in Eastern Europe, Asia, Africa, and the Middle East. That's when I felt comfortable bringing people back into my photos. Contemplating individuals and convincing them to be part of my portrait was very enriching. During two years of intermittent travel photography, I received zero rejections from people. There had to be something I was doing right. I could charm people, get total strangers to agree to pose, and give me the rights to their images. I even had my own exhibition of photos from Southeast Asia.

I now know why it was so easy for me to approach them successfully: They realized that their beauty, their presence, genuinely inspired me.

And that is irresistible.

As I connected with people through photography, I felt like connecting to organizations again. So, I started working with companies as an executive coach, 20 years after my first coaching training. Being in contact with people again, eager to connect, brought me an additional perspective that also became part of the inspirable model: the importance of the tribe.

My un-inspirable days were coming to an end.

Be In

Have you taken a long break from work? How has this changed the view of your context or your purpose? Please write down your ideas.

_____

_____

_____

_____

_____

_____

_____

_____

Chapter Insights

It was during the hard times of my transition that I started testing the limits of the traditional coaching approaches and finding the need to create new options. This gave birth to Step 1 of the Inspirable Way©: the Inspirable Self, the step where you start exploring the kind of person you want to be. This was not enough to navigate through all the difficulties of the transition:

- I realized the journey I was on was a very lonely one.
- I needed the support of a large tribe of inspirational people to inject joy into my development process.
- In the same way, I needed to contribute to the growth of those around me.

Chapter 10 - Step 2: The Tribe

Growth only happens when needed to overcome limitations.

You cannot rely on willpower to change.

Frequent contact with inspirational people makes growth joyful.

In my entire career dedicated to people development, I have found it pretty evident that the idea of changing something about ourselves doesn't just come out of the blue. Lounging in your Lay-Z-Boy in front of the screen, all snuggled up and comfortable in your favorite blanket, you probably won't get a random thought telling you to do a workout. When you realize you're having a hard time zipping up your pants, you may start making plans to join a gym.

Growth only happens, without exception, to overcome a limitation. Put differently, it is almost as if having to deal with an obstacle is the motivating factor that gets the ball rolling and makes us want to learn and change.

Let me explain this with one example from the professional environment. You may think of taking some courses so you can work on technology-related projects, but you've worked at your position for years and have seniority. You haven't really put in the effort to learn new things because you're in your comfort zone. Then you hear that there is going to be a layoff in your company and most of the vacancies require people who are tech savvy or familiar with agile ways of working. The next day, you sign up for the course you were postponing.

Maybe when you began your career, it was easy to stay on task and complete assignments that your boss gave you. You didn't worry about improving or changing things. Then you return from maternity leave to realize your time management skills are below par and the meetings and video calls don't seem to be helping. You start working with a younger team whose individuals are very familiar with chat and collaborative platforms such as Slack and Teams. When you see the difficulty in front of you, you get into action.

The traditional approach to personal growth

In large corporations, situations like this are when executive coaching kicks in. Its method (individually or with a team) is based on identifying the obstacle and creating an action plan. This usually requires a lot of reflection, which involves looking inside yourself during sometimes painful but productive sessions.

There are different kinds of coaches, such as the life coach who works with the individual to increase fulfillment in their personal and often spiritual lives, or the executive coach who specializes in business and career issues. They can help you improve your skills as well as manage stress. Getting this kind of help has been extremely useful to me in the past. My executive coach helped get me unstuck from some hard-coded behaviors such as excessive individualism and competitiveness. I have also been an executive coach myself and have seen many people getting closer to their goals because of my intervention.

The detriments of willpower

The downside of coaching is that we are not always in the mood or in the adequate stage of our lives to go through deep inner work to achieve our goals. In most self-development and growth processes, big change can be extremely painful because it relies on willpower. Emotions can run high during your first session. The coach helps you define who you want to be and what goals you want to achieve. You are joyful because you come out of the first session thinking: "Okay, I'm going to conquer the world! These are the kinds of things I've wanted to do for so many years and I have not done it. I'm ready now!"

These processes are about helping you realize what is happening in your life, which is a good thing, but then your joy slides down the scale because you become overwhelmed: "Wow, there are so many things that I need to fix about myself, so many things that I need to change."

Relaying on willpower doesn't work

When you become disillusioned is when the executive coach will ask you to stay committed. He tells you, "We will go through several sessions, and you are going to improve and achieve your goal at the end."

As a coach myself, I can tell you this is very hard, and many people will quit in the middle of the process. Why? Because besides managing many things in your life like work, family, finances, and wellness, on top of that you have to question yourself all the time in order to change. It drains all your willpower. *Drained people are not healthy, cheerful people.*

Most recent research has demonstrated the problems of relying on willpower[36]. Benjamin Hardy, the author of *Willpower Doesn't Work* states:

"

"According to psychological research, your willpower is like a muscle. It's a finite resource that is depleted with use. As a result, by the end of your strenuous days, your willpower muscles are exhausted and you're left to your naked and defenseless self—with zero control to stop the night-time munchies and time wasters."[37]

It is not difficult to understand that in the traditional development process, only the strongest get to the end, while the rest quit in the middle, feeling frustrated and guilty for their "lack of commitment."

It's a daunting experience, but you should not postpone your personal growth until you are in the right mood or have the right energy. So, how do you face your obstacles without feeling like you're doomed to fail?

---

[36] Benjamin Hardy. *Willpower Doesn't Work*, (New York: Hachette Books, 2018.)

[37] Benjamin Hardy. "Willpower Doesn't Work. Here's How to Actually Change Your Life." October 20, 2019. https://benjaminhardy.com/willpower-doesnt-work-heres-how-to-actually-change-your-life

Joy is the substitute of willpower

What if you could start a journey where your joy will grow with every step you take, a journey without action plans and deadlines? What if we could start a journey that is not asking you to leave your comfort zone, but instead make your comfort zone expand with every next move? What if this is a journey you don't have to do on your own but be accompanied by people who you look up to, who inspire you?

Sounds nice, right? Having companions is one of the fundamental differences that the Inspirable Way© has in comparison with traditional learning models. Companions are a source of joy, and joy is the substitute for willpower. This doesn't mean you should not spend time by yourself. It is just that your journey will be more joyful if you have frequent travel companions.

I am proposing a big mindset shift here: We have been raised to believe that pain and sacrifice will pay off in the end, and that joy is a word for hedonists. Fortunately, your limbic brain does not believe it; hence it constantly sabotages any project you have that involves meaningless effort or pain. Therefore, people quit meaningless jobs, stop painful, lonely workouts, or starving intermittently to death.

As you can see in Figure 6, the line that represents the Inspirable Way© demonstrates that growing along with others helps, you avoid the dip of traditional change models, keeping you engaged all the way.

By now, you might have already sketched out the first part of the exploration: who you want to become, Your Inspirable Self. You should have already pinpointed the areas of your life you want to improve, and even drafted some behaviors you want to change.

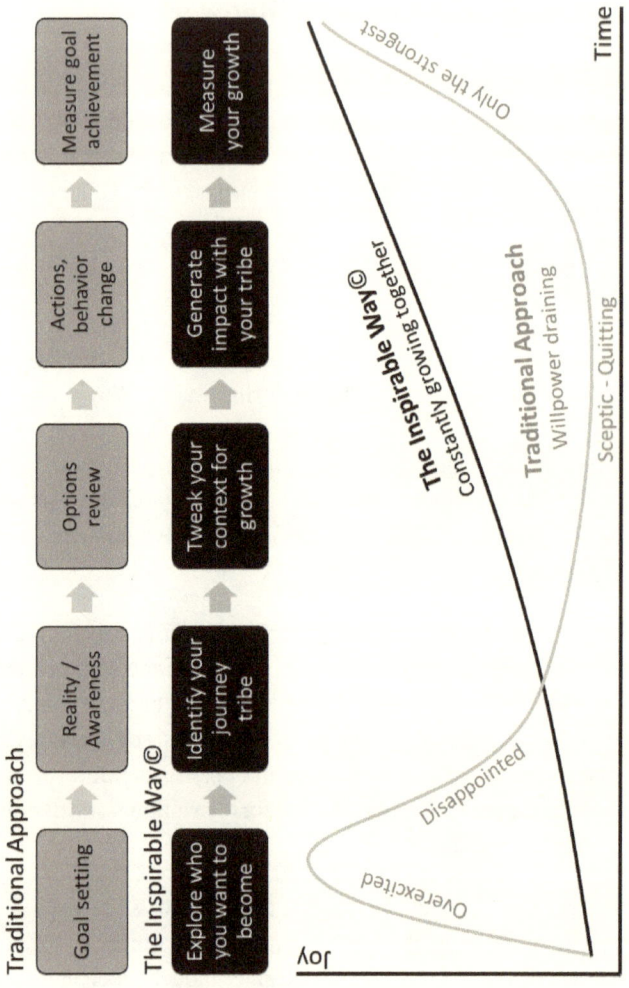

Figure 6: The Inspirable Way vs. traditional model comparison.

The Inspirable Way© is based on the premise that the type of people you are connected to plays a role in the definition of your growth as a person. You might have heard Jim Rohn's classic phrase, "You are the average of the five people you spend the most time with."[38] Dr. David McClelland, Harvard social psychologist, said, "The people you habitually associate with determine as much as 95 percent of your success or failure in life."[39]

Social contagion is the phenomenon that involves the spreading of behaviors and emotions spontaneously through the interaction taking place within a group of people. French polymath Gustave Le Bon coined this term in his 1895 work *The Crowd: A Study of the Popular Mind*[40].

Although Le Bon already included the condition of spontaneity in his definition, a century later in year 1993, American psychologists David A. Levy and Paul R. Nail expanded the social contagion definition to "the spread of affect, attitude or behavior where the recipient does not perceive an intentional influence attempt on the part of the initiator."[41]

There are two types of social contagion:

The simple one is where the individual needs only one interaction to start imitating the behaviors. An example of this can be when the individual goes to a government office, sees the queue, and immediately gets in line with no need for instructions.

---

[38] Doorn, Maarten van. 'You Are the Average Of The Five People You Spend The Most Time With'. Medium (blog), 17 June 2019.
https://maartenvandoorn.medium.com/you-are-the-average-of-the-five-people-you-spend-the-most-time-with-a2ea32d08c72

[39] Darren Hardy. *The Compound Effect: Jumpstart Your Income, Your Life, Your Success*. (SUCCESS Books, 2010.)

[40] Gustave Le Bon. *The Crowd: A Study of the Popular Mind*. 1895.

[41] David Levy and Paul Nail. "Contagion: A Theoretical and Empirical Review and Reconceptualization." *Genetic, Social, and General Psychology Monographs* 119 (June 1, 1993): 233–84.

The complex one is where the individual needs to be in contact with multiple sources, especially close friends, to make imitation legitimate. For example, you join a meditation course where some friends are already taking part.

Complex social contagion is the phenomenon that supports the thesis behind the Inspirable Way©: If you identify a group of people whose behaviors you would like to adopt, not only you will absorb those habits, but you will also copy their emotions and attitudes with a minimum effort. The importance of making this a conscious decision is because this trait works positively if you chose the right people, but if you are not managing this and end up spending most of your time with people who behave in a way that harms your growth, you might be infected, as well.

Tribes

In your case, who are these people you spend most of your time with? Who is your tribe? To how many tribes do you belong to? You might ask yourself, why am I talking about tribes right now?

The "tribe" is a concept described as one of the most important enablers or blockers in your personal development. British anthropologist Robin Dunbar coined the modern concept of a tribe in the workplace. He stated that although in the modern world we are connected with thousands of people, in reality, we can only maintain relations with about 150 maximum.[42] This covers every aspect of our lives, from personal relationships to work ones. If you think about it, we need to be really careful who these 150 people are. As social contagion happens mostly

---

[42] "Dunbar's Number: Why We Can Only Maintain 150 Relationships." 2019. https://www.bbc.com/future/article/20191001-dunbars-number-why-we-can-only-maintain-150-relationships

within tribes, development spreads quicker when you belong to one or many.

Of course, in our 21st-century world, we don't only belong to one tribe; we belong to many tribes. We are part of the tribe of our business unit at work, and part of the tribe that goes to the same gym. We belong to a tribe of parents at our children's school, and we might belong to a salsa dancers' tribe.

But nowadays, when you belong to a tribe, you might not be connected to all the people in that tribe, only some. Somehow, with the groups of people you engage with in each tribe you belong to, you create your own tribe.

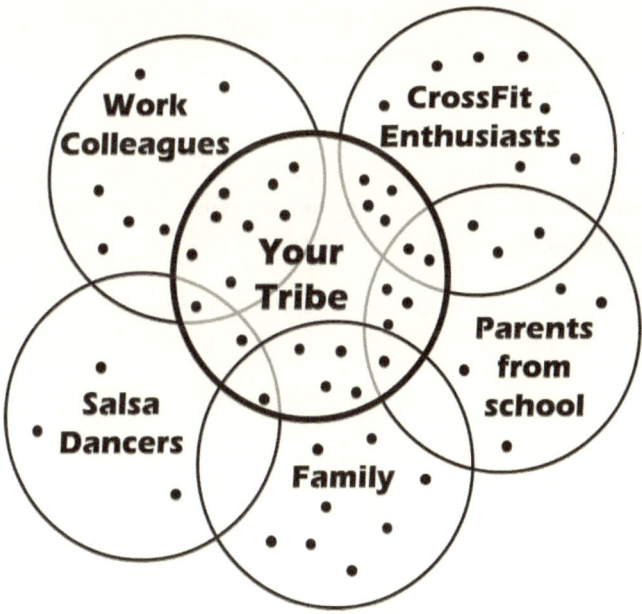

Figure 7: A tribe of tribes.

So, if you are a teenager and you hang around with friends who smoke, you are very likely to end up smoking. It doesn't matter if you work on your confidence. It's too difficult not to follow what your tribe is doing. That's why they say if you want to quit something like drinking, you need to avoid the friends who do. It requires too much willpower to avoid the temptation; too many easy triggers will destroy any self-improvement plans.

The good news is that this concept works especially well from a positive angle. If you want to be healthier and you are surrounded by people who do yoga, eat vegetarian and fresh meals, go hiking, ride bikes, or work out at the gym, you'll be more likely to do the same. It will actually be difficult not to care about being healthy.

When you identify the people in your tribe, you realize that most of them are not there to inspire you, but you need to guarantee that at least some of them do. When I was reviewing my tribe, I realized I had people who I had an inspirational relationship with, but I also identified other types of relationships:

- Some friends who I had a **supportive** relationship with.
- Others, like my parents, with whom I had a **love** relationship.
- Some acquaintances from my daughter's school who I had a **coordination** relationship with.
- Many combinations of the previous groups.

Identify your tribe

In the following exercise, I'm going to ask you to think only about those people in your tribe who inspire you. These are friends and family who impress or influence you with some things that they do in their daily lives. This could be your aunt who runs her own business or a co-worker who always seems to be organized. It could be a friend who is a brilliant father and spends quality time with his children. Remember, these people are not from a single tribe; they belong to the different tribes you belong to, but you will identify them as *your tribe*.

Take your tablet or a piece of paper, and make a drawing like the one shown here, or go to www.beinspirable.com and download the free workbook so that you can work directly in the diagrams.

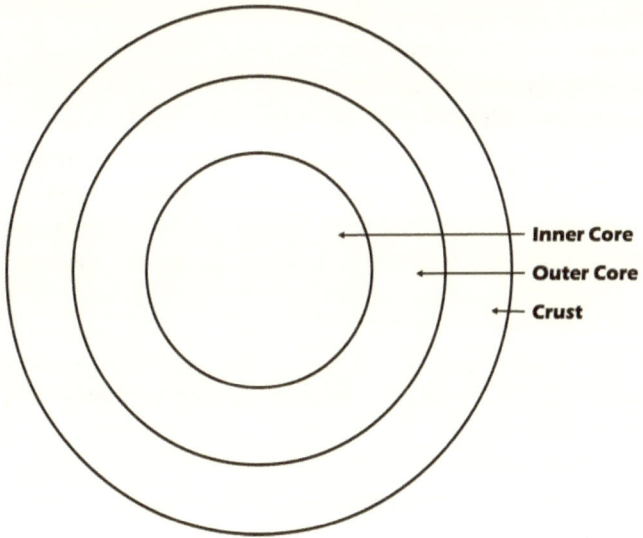

Figure 8: The three levels of a tribe.

This is going to be your inspirational tribe map. As you can see, I split it into three levels:

Inner Core. Here you will include the names of the people that are very close to you, who you trust, and who know about your successes, failures, and struggles. These are typically people who would come to your birthday party. Most of them you see or communicate with on a daily or weekly basis. They know your moods, emotions, habits, and battles.

Outer Core. The people with whom you might have a strong bond but you are not in frequent contact with them will belong here. It could be, for example, someone who used to be your teacher and now you only see her maybe every few months or someone you went to college with but now only hear from during the holidays. They don't know much about your successes and struggles.

Crust. These are people who you have met and have made a positive impression on. Even though you don't have a deep connection with them, they could be a role model for your areas of development. Maybe a consultant you met who has already published two books, or it could be an accountant you met at a party who seemed to give solid financial advice. Even limited exposure to these people can affect the way you live your life.

I want to share with you one of the first diagrams I made for myself when I was creating this framework. I took the three layers of my tribe and I divided them into my three main areas of development: to be healthy, to be joyful, and to take part in interesting projects. Remember, when it is your turn to do it, to include your two, three, or four development areas.

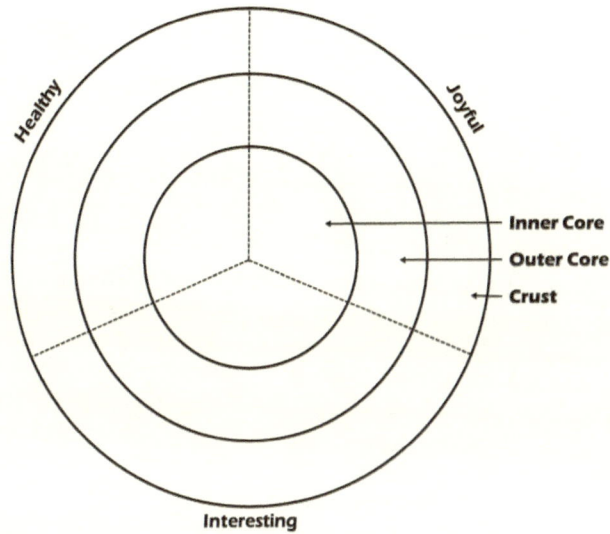

Figure 9: Tribe split by development areas.

With this in mind, I started including the people I thought could inspire me in each area, those who could influence my behavior for the better. You can see what I came up with in Figure 10.

It was no simple task, and after I did my first run, I stopped, as I preferred to sleep on it. The next day I had a more independent view and it helped me remember the names of more people who have brought me loads of inspiration. Just by doing it, I felt more confident about my intentions.

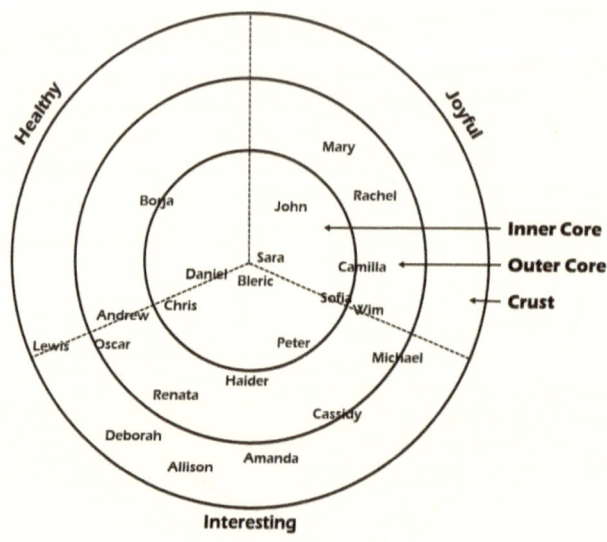

Figure 10: Tribe members.

I also had interesting findings. There are some areas in my diagram that are completely empty. I could list many people in the "interesting" category at every level of my tribe. But in the "healthy" portion and, to a lesser extent, in the "joyful" one, I had a hard time coming up with people who weren't close to my inner core. Why? Because, until recently, being joyful and healthy was not at the forefront of my mind. I was mostly focused on professional goals.

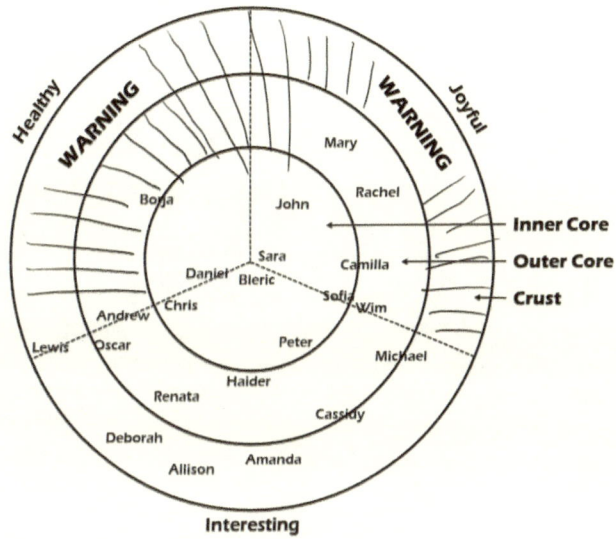

Figure 11: Empty areas of the tribe.

Also, I realized that some people that were in outer layers could be brought closer to my core with simple actions like inviting them for a coffee or asking for their advice on a specific project. If you want to be inspirable, you need to have inspirational people in your tribe, and the closer you have them, the better.

In many conversations with people who do this exercise, they felt the urge to act to bring closer those who are in the farthest orbits of their system. If this is your case, let me tell you that Step 4: the Inspirable Moves, is completely dedicated to this. If you want to experiment now because you see some quick wins happening, please go ahead!

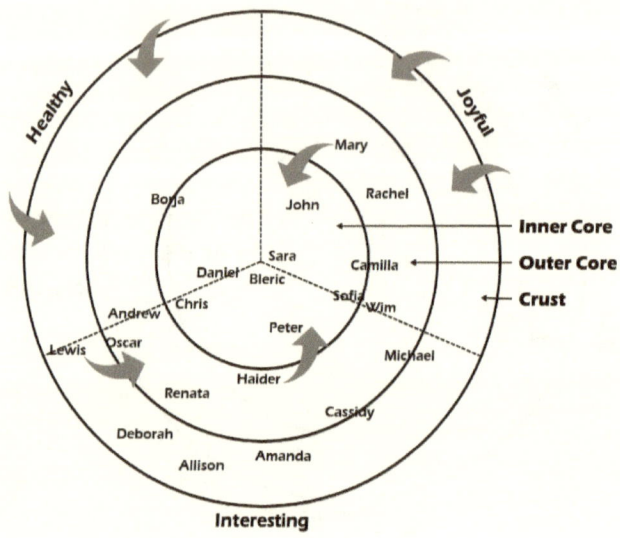

Figure 12: Bringing members closer to the core.

To define these actions, take advantage of the wisdom of Harvard professors Robert Kegan and Lisa Lahey[43] who recommend actions that follow a SMART structure. This is a completely different acronym than the one typically used millions of times to set performance objectives[44]:

---

[43] Robert Kegan and Lisa Laskow Lahey. *Immunity to Change: How to Overcome It and Unlock the Potential in Yourself and Your Organization (Leadership for the Common Good.* (Boston: Harvard Business Review Press, 2009.)

[44] The performance objective SMART acronym means: Specific, Measurable, Achievable, Relevant, and Time-bound.

Safe. If it is too risky, you might not even start.

Modest. If you go too ambitious, it will drain your willpower and your joy.

Actionable. You can start doing it right now, no excuses.

Research purpose. By doing it, you will learn about yourself and about your intentions.

Test-oriented. It will help you prove if you are on the right track.

These were my actions for experimenting:

Person	Area	Action
Cassidy	Interesting projects	Ask her for feedback on the Inspirable methodology.
Andrew	Interesting projects	Do more research on NFTs to initiate conversations on the subject.
People in the gym	Health	Getting to know by name two or three more people in the gym.
My wife Bleric and my daughter Sara	Joyful	We created a summer reading club which meant many lovely nights in our living room.

Table 3: Exploratory actions.

In my initial actions, I did not cover the Joyful area. This is OK. Again, this is not a stressful practice where you need to come out of your comfort zone. A couple of months later, once my comfort zone had expanded enough, I started including activities in my list.

Be In

Draw your three layers diagram and divide the circles according to the areas of interest that you have identified. Include the people that inspire you in each of the areas. Analyze your diagram: any empty areas? Any overcrowded areas? Write down your thoughts.

_____

_____

_____

_____

_____

_____

_____

_____

Chapter Insights

This chapter unlocks the core differentiator of the Inspirable Way©, sustainable _personal growth happens when we surround ourselves with inspirational people_ whose sole presence makes us jump off of the couch and get into action.

- You need to identify who these people are. You can do it in the provided three-layer diagram that you can split into your two or three development areas. Remember, this is not to identify all the people that belong to your network; _only the people who inspire you are part of this map._ You can download the diagrams used in this chapter in our website: www.beinspirable.com

- Doing this exercise will make you own and start taking care of your Inspirable Tribe.
- You will be tempted to start contacting people you did not have on your radar; please do so! Our gut feelings with these initiatives work well most of the time.

Keep in mind that Step 4 of this model is about actions to increase your engagement with your tribe, so, if you prefer to wait and have more information before acting, it's your choice, as usual.

Chapter 11 - A Conscious Journey

What do you fear losing the most?

Have you had any online group learning experience that transformed you?

How has technology contributed to your personal growth?

While I was a child, a student, and even during the beginning of my professional career, I was naturally inspirable. Without thinking about it, I looked for people I loved and respected to show me how to act, think, and behave. I was instinctively searching for someone to inspire me to do great things. Then when I worked for a company where I failed to create a growth environment for myself, I lost my inspirable condition.

Once I freed myself from that suffocating situation, I now had to figure out how to be inspirable again. This would be my journey to become Consciously Inspirable, and as I have mentioned in previous chapters, executive coaching turned out to be the first step of the way.

Who Learns More, the Coach or the Coachee?

Coaching in the business world is a tough job, and at the same time, a very rewarding experience. People who are really into coaching, like my good friend Sofia Victor[45], get rewarded through the satisfaction of helping others and also the learning they get during the session. In my case, every session as a coach was a learning experience for me, as well. By helping people sort out their problems, I was also learning how to get myself unstuck.

I coached for about two years, working with employees from different companies, as well as executives who were recently fired from several big tech companies. This last assignment was key for me: I worked with dozens of highly paid executives in transition. They had many things in common:

- All of them had an idea of what they wanted to do next: get employed, start a new company, or retire.
- They were focused on the result they wanted to achieve, but not on who they wanted to become. They had difficulties defining their future identity, as I did.
- All of them felt disconnected from the newer generations. They complained a lot about their behaviors and their values.
- They were terrified of losing their status in society, although their talk was always about the opposite. Their status made it difficult for them to explore out-of-the-box options.

Although some of them were really prepared for a big change in their lives, their immediate circle was not: spouses, daughters, sons, and parents had certain needs and expectations.

[45] Sofia Victor is the founder of Connecting Dots, a successful coaching entrepreneurship in Spain.. https://www.connecting-dots.es

They relied on the money-makers and could not let that system go so easily. This kept my clients isolated and attached to old ideas and ways of thinking. They could not learn new things. Fear kept them un-inspirable. I can relate to how they were feeling as I went through the same situation.

As a coach, I was helping these executives get their answers, but they were so lonely walking down that path that they frequently broke down and needed to take weeks off. This was so hard on them that they usually needed to take several months to complete their sessions. In terms of success, few transformed themselves. Most of them would just survive the dip, gain some self-confidence back, and go on with their lives similar to before. If they were lucky, they would find a lower-paid job that kept them on a payroll until retirement.

So, I kept pushing myself; there has to be a way to make this easier for people, less painful! We cannot continue in the 21st century with the "work hard" approach. We need to move once and for all to the "work smart" approach, and even beyond that, we need to have fun while we are doing it.

And then, while I was looking for options to solve this problem, I had an experience that provided me with one part of the answer. In the year 2014, I decided to update my coaching training and I discovered my first MOOC.

What is a MOOC? It is a Massive Open Online Course. This one was called *Unlocking the Immunity to Change*. It was an experiment created by Harvard University and edX[46], an open course platform now part of 2U. This free program about personal change was designed by professors Robert Kegan and Lisa Lahey, who have been studying for decades people's resistance to stick to medical treatments, even in situations

---

[46] edX has been one of the main MOOC platforms. https://www.edx.org/

where not following the recommendations could lead to death. Kegan and Lahey brought their approach from the health sector to the corporate world, using a MOOC to test the level of interest by the public.

60,000 people inspiring each other

The program duration was 14 weeks and more than 60,000 people signed in. It was an amazing experience to be connected with people around the world. Can you imagine thousands of people sharing concerns, frustrations, and limitations in open forums?

My insight after completing the program was that even though the methodology was great, straightforward, and easy to understand and apply, the most important part was we did it together, thousands of people together. Initially, we were all anonymous, but we started connecting; week after week, I knew more names of people that were on the same journey that I was on.

The difference with my coaching processes was that during the MOOC, every day I was looking forward to connecting. I was not using my willpower and I was not drained. Quite the opposite: I gained more energy after every contact.

After 14 weeks, I gained self-confidence again, not supported by a method but supported by others. I recently heard Simon Sinek being interviewed by Lewis Howes in The School of Greatness podcast[47] and he said self-confidence doesn't come

---

[47] Lewis Howes. "4 Habits That Will Make You Unstoppable." The School of Greatness. January 7, 2022. Podcast Ep. 1212.
https://lewishowes.com/podcast/4-habits-that-will-make-you-unstoppable/

from the inside. "Children are not born self-confident; their confidence is built by their parents, their friends, their teachers." In my case, a 60,000 people tribe nourished it.

I got a seed from the Unlocking Immunity to Change experience that I wanted to plant. The power is in the tribe, not in the method. This guided me to develop how I wanted to help people.

The Immunity to Change MOOC helped thousands without the need of a coach. I realized that technology has to be part of the equation if I want to have a big impact.

Be In

Think about people you know who are making big changes in their lives. What do you like about how they are doing it?

_____

_____

_____

_____

_____

_____

_____

After this training, I traveled to Boston to get certified as a facilitator of the *Immunity to Change* methodology. It was a wonderful seminar and I still use the technique today to support any employee, student, or team that wants to change and grow. I always include the tribe as the crucial element to enable evolution in a joyful, sustainable way.

Chapter Insights

Fear of losing is one of the major causes to become un-inspirable, and this fear usually stays there even when you have lost that thing you regarded, like your job.

- When you are frightened and insecure, it is very difficult to start a transformation journey on your own. Even with the help of a personal coach, you will gain self-awareness but it will require lots of willpower to get to the end.
- The key to joyful growth is to keep constant contact with your inspirable tribe, those whose behavior makes you to become a better person.
- You can make this process even more enriching if you improve your environment, as well.

The next chapter is about how you can tweak your context to make it contribute to your development.

Chapter 12 - Step 3: The Context

How does your current context contribute to your personal growth?

How does your environment affect your organization and your emotions?

How easy is it to change your current setting?

A few pages ago, we explored the importance of building a tribe. You might have done the first identification of the people in your tribe whose behaviors could inspire you to grow in certain areas of your life.

The tribe is the core of the Inspirable Way©, but, as you will see, your environment plays a key role in your blooming process. You need a proper habitat, an Inspirable Context. This place has to be as motivational and encouraging as your tribe, as well as an additional enabler to your dreams and vision. For the sake of understanding it and cultivating it properly, I have divided it into four dimensions.

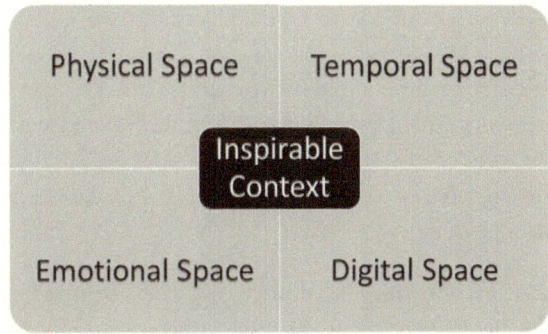

Figure 13: Four dimensions of your Inspirable Context.

Physical space

This is the space where we spend most of our time during the day. It includes your home, your workplace, and, if you commute daily, your car or another transportation method.

We usually share this space with other people, such as our families and our colleagues, so we might not be able to transform them according to our sole wishes, but most of the time, *just tweaking it is enough.* By the way, I usually prefer the concept of tweaking to transforming. Why? We can act sooner and see if what we did works. If it does, then tweak some more. Constant tweaking in a short period can cause a huge transformation.

Of course, what you decide to tweak will depend on the areas you have identified you want to improve. It is not the same to tweak your home to make it a healthier place than to make it a more organized one or a leisure-oriented area. The same applies to your workplace. The changes you introduce to your office will be completely different if you need a cozier environment oriented toward creativity than if you are looking for one fully oriented to foster conversations.

To decide on what to tweak in your physical space, I would like to introduce you to a concept from James Clear[48], an expert in the science of building positive habits and getting rid of negative ones. His approach is very simple: Take care of your context (your context), make sure it facilitates the activities you want to do more of, and makes more difficult the habits you want to stop doing.

He calls this friction. You design your context to reduce the friction for the behaviors you want to boost and increase the friction of the ones you want to reduce. I definitely recommend this approach to review your physical space.

Here are some examples I have gathered from many people in different areas of improvement:

Area of Personal Improvement	Proposed tweaks
Efficiency	Remove distractions and unnecessary objects to reduce visual clutter. You might laugh, but Netflix phenomenon Marie Kondo's rules of basic tidying work great here: • Organize stuff by category: clothing, books, sentimental items. • Start discarding distracting stuff by each category, and don't skip to the next category until you've finished the previous one. Do it all in one go. • Keep only those things that still spark joy.
Health	Although health is a complex subject, here are some examples: • Organize your food in your kitchen, with healthier stuff very visible at eye level. Keep

---

48 James Clear. *Atomic Habits: An Easy & Proven Way to Build Good Habits & Break Bad Ones*. (New York: Avery, 2018.)

	unhealthier stuff out of reach and especially out of sight. • Your workout/running/yoga clothing have to be handy, always clean, and ready to wear. • Include motivational messages around you. This might sound corny, but you will start believing that you are becoming a healthier person, and that's the trick.
Family	Make sure you have enough places to meet each other frequently. Maybe the kitchen and the dining room are not enough. If your space is not huge, then you might need to trade some individual spaces for family ones or even create some flexible spaces. For example, adapting a room so that you can use it as your home office during the day and for playing board games during the weekend.
Learning	This one is very close to my heart: In our home you will see books everywhere. We also read digital, but we wanted paper books because we liked them to remind ourselves (and our daughter) of the pleasure of continuous self-improvement. And where there is a book, there is a comfortable couch to sit on and read. We still have a TV, but now we use it only once a week to have our pizza-and-movie Friday night. We might eventually get rid of it, as it is not aligned with our personal growth plans anymore.

Table 4: Tweaking by area of improvement.

Temporal space

When we think about space, we tend to think only about physical space. In my case, as an avid sci-fi reader, I always kept in mind the fourth dimension: Time.

As corporate animals, entrepreneurship animals, business animals, we are used to planning our time in the most important tool of our smartphone or computer: the calendar.

My favorite guru in optimizing the use of time is Israeli-born American author and lecturer Nir Eyal[49]. He recommends the following order to do the planning of your week:

1. **Yourself**, the first step. Everything that is related to yourself and your basic needs. He recommends that in your calendar you should book your visits to the gym and also the time allocated to eat and sleep. Not so long ago, I set a daily alarm that shows me it is time to go to sleep. It has been my only way to guarantee 7+ hours of sleep every night.

2. **Relationships**, the second step. You need to include in your calendar all the time you want to spend with the people who matter to you, including the ones closest to you, like your spouse and children. It might sound excessive, but if it's not in there, other priorities will swiftly take over. I spend a lot of time with my daughter, but Wednesdays after school are special: We go for a snack together at a lovely bakery she loves, I turn off my phone for two hours, and all my attention goes to our conversation or the occasional card game. Breakfasts during weekends are the time for special conversations with my wife, which usually start way before our daughter wakes up.

3. **Work**, the last step. Of course, you need to book time for work. The trick is to keep it to specific, define timeslots for the different tasks that you need to get done, time for meetings, and unplanned time for contingencies. Since the pandemic lockdown, I avoided setting one-hour meetings because I ended up frequently involved in back-to-back meetings. Now I prefer to book 30-, 45-, or 90-minute

---

[49] Nir Eyal. *Indistractable: How to Control Your Attention and Choose Your Life*. (Dallas, TX: BenBella Books, 2019.)

meetings, guaranteeing many breaks during the day. My trick is, I'm always the one who sends the invitations.

Be In

According to your areas of improvement, which are activities that you need to include regularly in your calendar? Make sure you are thinking about the three levels: You, Relations, Work.

_____

_____

_____

_____

_____

_____

Eyal's philosophy is that when you book time for an activity, be it a meeting or spending time with your daughter, you need to do it without distractions. Science has proved that humans are not good at multitasking:

"There is a sense of pride often felt when multitasking, as if we have defied human nature by completing more than one high-level brain task at a time, rendering us both superhuman and incredibly efficient. There are various actions we can engage in simultaneously that are not considered multitasking—walking and talking, for example. Multitasking is defined as the act of completing more than one task at the same time—such as studying for an exam while cooking dinner or sending emails while watching the news. The hard neurological truth, however, is that we are not multitasking. Rather, we are toggling back and forth between two tasks. In many cases, we would be more efficient if we, instead, single-tasked while also creating a conscious start and stop to each task."[50]

Avoiding distractions seems like an insurmountable challenge, especially having in your pocket the biggest source of all: the mobile phone. Managing your digital space becomes a priority.

Digital space

The digital space is all that time that we spend actively connected to the Internet: browsing websites, checking social media apps, text, audio, and video messaging, emailing, online banking, food ordering, looking for directions, listening to podcasts, watching movies and series, dating and so much more.

The Internet has increased our productivity to levels we never dreamed of a couple of decades ago, but it has also increased our anxiety and distraction levels.

I will not recommend that you spend less time online, but I will use again the wisdom of Nir Eyal to say that you should get

---

[50] Shonda Moralis and Sarah Dinan. "The Myth of Multitasking." *Psychology Today*. February 27, 2022. https://www.psychologytoday.com/intl/blog/the-therapeutic-perspective/202202/the-myth-multitasking

online with intention[51]. Let me elaborate more on this: If you are writing a report and you need to do some research online to get some evidence for your argument, you are getting online with an intention. If you feel a little tired and you take a break to watch TikTok on your mobile for a few minutes, you are also doing it with an intention. You have consciously decided it.

What you need to avoid is falling into the trap: You are researching references for your report and you end up browsing TikTok or you were about to do your reference research and you check your email first instead. This is what Eyal calls distractions: when you do something without an intention, just following an impulse.

Distractions exist for many reasons: maybe the task that you are trying to get done is too difficult, maybe you are anxious because you think you will fail, or sometimes it is just plain FOMO[52], you are trying to be everywhere simultaneously and multitasking again.

There are many ways to tackle this. When I need to do concentration work, I take my mobile out of my visual field and I keep only one program and one tab open at a time. If I'm writing or reading, I use the "focused" mode on the computer to avoid interruptions via chat or email notifications. If I need extreme focus, I do an additional 10-minute "focus" meditation in the Headspace app before I start, and then I wear earplugs or noise-canceling headphones during work.

---

[51] Lewis Howes. "Build Life Changing Habits & Become a Productivity Master with Nir Eyal." The School of Greatness. April 14, 2021. Podcast Ep. 1097. https://lewishowes.com/podcast/build-life-changing-habits-become-a-productivity-master-with-nir-eyal
[52] 'Fear of Missing Out'. Wikipedia. February 9, 2022. https://en.wikipedia.org/w/index.php?title=Fear_of_missing_out&oldid=1070836413

There is one thing most experts agree on: You can only successfully stay in focus for short periods, after which our productivity drops. The Pomodoro approach is based on this assumption to keep you focused on one subject at a time in 25-minute time slots. It has a very simple app[53] for free. Try it!

In case we become distracted and find ourselves online browsing, there are ways to make sure that at least we are consuming the best content for us. Nowadays there is a lot on the news blaming algorithms for our distractions[54], but we can try to make the algorithms to work our way. Imagine that you are interested in your personal development. Maybe you should start following entrepreneur Lewis Howes[55] in the different social networks. If you are interested in neuroscience, follow Dr. Andrew D. Huberman[56], and if you are interested in what's going on in Silicon Valley, maybe you need to check *New York Times* journalist Kara Swisher.[57] The algorithm will understand these are your preferences and will start proposing loads of similar interesting people to follow.

If you want to use social networks for personal growth and for entertainment, I suggest you create separate accounts for each purpose. I do this and I get entertainment-related

---

[53] "Pomodoro® Timer Web App." Francesco Cirillo: Work Smarter, Not Harder. Accessed February 14, 2022.
https://francescocirillo.com/products/pomodoro-timer-web-app
[54] An algorithm is a set of instructions for solving a problem or accomplishing a task. One common example of an algorithm is a recipe, which consists of specific instructions for preparing a dish or meal. When this concept is taken to the digital environment, one of the problems that mostly discussed about the algorithms in social networks is that they are constantly analyzing the type of content that you consume the most, and then it is supposed to provide you more of that type of content. That in itself is not bad, but there are many who are filing legal claims that these algorithms are biased and bring more and more radical content to our apps, which is raising the level of polarization in our societies.
[55] https://twitter.com/LewisHowes
[56] https://twitter.com/hubermanlab
[57] https://twitter.com/karaswisher

recommendations on my personal account and professional suggestions on the other.

Be In

Who are you going to start following in your social networks to help you grow? Who are you going to stop following?

_____

_____

_____

_____

_____

_____

_____

Emotional space

As the day goes by, we experiment with many different emotions. Some experts talk about the existence of 6 or 7 basic emotions, which usually include anger, fear, disgust, happiness, sadness, and surprise, but if you search on the Internet, you will find opinions that talk about 27 emotional states, or 50 or 100. This is not wrong; it is just that some experts dive more into the details and nuances of emotions, while others prefer to stay at a higher level, studying the implications they have in our daily lives. If you are not a psychologist, having a basic understanding of the six emotions that I mentioned will be enough to take you through this section.

Regardless of the categorization, most experts concur that there are no good or bad emotions. We need them all for different reasons, and we should not block any emotion from happening. Some emotions traditionally considered negative, such as sadness and anger, have their benefits; the first one provides an adequate platform for reflection and the second one helps you move into action.

I think when we want to grow in different areas of our life to become our Inspirable Selves, we need to favor the emotions that we would like to happen more frequently. If you want to become a motivational speaker, being sad all the time won't help you, but maybe some sadness could come in handy if you are a fictional drama writer.

How do we do this without involving therapy? Creating an emotional context that fosters the emotions you would like to feel more often.

If you want to feel energetic, you might need to include Pop or Latin music in your Spotify playlist. You could use lively colors in your decoration. Maybe neon lights are too much, but you get the point. The temperature in your environment cannot be too warm, as excessive coziness will get you to sit on your couch and even take a nap. You don't want that, as you want to feel active, so keep it cool and you'll stay on the move.

From a different perspective, if you need to have more of a thoughtful mood, you might include Bossa nova or Chill-out music in your playlist. Calmer, warmer colors you can find in nature should surround you. You can keep your environment warmer to keep it cozier, but again keep in mind that if it gets too warm, you will lie on the couch for hours watching Netflix and not being productive. If it gets too cold, you'll do the same but with a blanket.

Another important element to creating an emotional space aligned with your development needs is your language.

- If you use too much negativity in your wording, it will be very hard to become more optimistic.
- Spending too much time talking about the past will limit your possibilities to build a promising future.
- Talking too much and listening very little will get you focused only on your problems, and you will miss all the great learning opportunities the world brings.

Modifying the way you talk can be difficult, but I suggest starting small. Aim to eliminate any word or expression from your vocabulary that is not aligned with your desired behaviors. Monitor your language for a few weeks until you are sure you have gotten rid of it, and when you are sure, you can try getting rid of another expression.

It is always beneficial to nominate a trustworthy person to tell you what you should change about your language and verify your progress.

Be In

What do you need to adjust in your emotional space? Think about, music, colours, objects and your language.

_____

_____

_____

_____

_____

_____

_____

Chapter Insights

Having identified your Inspirable Tribe, you need to find ways to bring its members closer to you. This will immediately expose you to people and ideas that are aligned with what you want in your life. This is not the hunter's approach where you set one goal for yourself and do everything you can to make it happen within the deadline. Instead, this is the explorer's approach, where the journey itself will bring you closer to the person you want to become. Beware, as the exploration itself will modify that image of the person you want to become. This is a good thing because it means you are being flexible. This way you will face no frustration, as you will look forward to the journey's continuation.

The Inspirable Way© is a lifestyle, and Step 3: The Inspirable Context makes your development process smoother. How?

- Making sure your environment facilitates the incorporation of new behaviors aligned with your aim and making it tougher for misaligned habits to survive.
- There is a key word in this step, "tweak," which means you don't need to make big changes in your environment. Implement small constant tweaks and you will speed up your growth.
- When we think about our environment, only the physical context comes to our mind. We need to make it a priority to tweak our temporal, digital, and emotional domains. This is not a one-time tweak but incorporating a constant tweaking habit.

Chapter 13 - Became Inspirable, Became Digital

Are you seizing most of the opportunities the digital world offers?

When was the last time you thought "out of the box"?

How did the COVID-19 pandemic change the way you see the world?

The digital space is a source of distractions but is also the biggest source of opportunities to grow. Taking part in the *Unlocking the Immunity to Change* MOOC, along with 60K people for 14 weeks, helped me see this clearly. This digital opportunity was the gateway to a completely new tribe that I could not access before.

It is difficult to pinpoint the benefits that connecting to a new tribe has, but I can definitely say excitement is one of them.

When the *Unlocking the Immunity to Change* MOOC ended, I contacted Minds at Work[58] to sign up to become a facilitator of its framework. I became part of one of the initial groups the

---

[58] Minds at Work is the company that created the Immunity to Change Approach founded by Robert Kegan and Lisa Lahey. https://mindsatwork.com/

company was training. I traveled to Boston during the fall of 2014, and thanks to the wonders of Airbnb, I could easily rent a comfortable basement of a large house on Harvard Street, just a 10-minute walk from the university campus. During the workshop I met interesting people from different backgrounds and generations, but I met the most fascinating individuals when the workshop was finished and my reconnection with the tech and digital world started.

Every morning during the Immunity to Change trainings, I had breakfast at IHOP near Harvard Square, which has been my favorite breakfast place since my childhood years. One day at the restaurant, I overheard a group of students having a conversation about "people analytics and social sensing technology." It seemed like something I wanted to know more about. I joined their conversation, and I asked them where I could get more information about it. They mentioned the name Ben Waber, the author of *People Analytics: How Social Sensing Technology Will Transform Business and What It Tells Us about the Future of Work.*

At MIT, Waber and his team developed a wearable technology that could objectively measure different variables within the workplace, such as leadership influence, team cohesion, and people engagement. This was done by recording the behavior of people while they were carrying a "sociometric badge", a device similar size of any company ID badge, just thicker and heavier, so you could still wear it around your neck and it was visible on your chest. The badge recorded motion, closeness to other people, tone of voice, and pitch.

Later, Waber co-founded Humanyze along with Tamie Kim and Daniel Olguin[59], a company that used this technology to

---

[59] Humanyze is the startup founded in 2010 by Ben Waber, Daniel Olguin, and Taemie Kim. https://humanyze.com/

improve leadership, teamwork, and the layout of workplaces to boost collaboration.

This was definitely ahead of its time, and since I've always loved the new and the bold, it caught my attention immediately. If this was true, it could bring a real scientific approach to leadership development.

I flew back home and told my wife that I wanted our company (mIDentity[60]) to be the first one to have this technology in Europe. So together we contacted Humanyze and talked to them about piloting its program in Spain. They included us among the potential partners, and we started planning the next steps.

Things moved fast. More happened in two months than in two years. During this short time, I was introduced by a colleague to a charming man from Belgium, Wim, who was also an experienced HR professional. We connected immediately, and after a few conversations, I asked him if he wanted to be part of the project with Humanyze. He said yes without hesitation.

It was interesting and enlightening to see how Wim approached things. He was a few years older than me, and sometimes his view of what the workplace should be was extremely disruptive, with his way of expressing it so politically incorrect that he left no one neutral. He was perfect for a disruptive project.

A few weeks later, we traveled to Boston to sign the agreement with Humanyze and bring the first batch of sociometric badges to Europe. But we were not the only company on the continent that was going to have it.

---

[60] https://www.midentity.tech/

Meet TAO Leadership

Humanyze chose two partners in Europe for the pilot: our company in Spain, mIDentity and TAO Leadership from the UK.

We connected immediately with the founders of TAO, Haider and Justin, and rather than becoming competitors, we started a journey together to learn about this tool. We executed many pilots with different companies. We created a model to train salespeople using the badges to provide feedback on how they were doing with interactions with potential customers[61].

In this period, we realized that the technology was ready to provide scientific information about leadership and teamwork, but most of the companies we dealt with were not ready for so much honesty. The fear of "what are you going to do with my data" was already growing in our society.

After a two-year period, although neither we nor TAO Leadership continued as partners with Humanyze, there was a before and an after regarding everything we knew about leadership and team behavior, and afterward both companies continued the exploration of technology solutions for human problems.

This journey gave me two inspiring friends, Wim and Haider.

Wim taught me to always to be open and to share knowledge, not to hide things, and to believe that there are no competitors, only collaborators. With him, I understood the real value of being connected to other people, not for networking but for the inspiration.

---

[61] In partnership with Grupo Persona in Spain.
https://grupopersona.es/

Years later he gave me an opportunity to become inspirable. Wim became the academic director of a Talent Development master's program at IE University[62], one of the most prestigious business schools in the world. He invited me to be part of the group of professors he was assembling for the masters, which I happily accepted.

Haider showed that high tech and high touch were not exclusive to each other. But the most important thing I learned from him was, you can run a business and stay true to your values. Aside from his futuristic approach to transform the workplace, Haider inspires because he stands for what he believes is right, which means openly supporting diversity and inclusion initiatives including LGBTQ+ and Black Lives Matter. Although he has never mentioned it to me, it is obvious that generosity and kindness are among his core principles. I believe that his ideals also have been key for expanding the TAO Leadership dream.

The Gift of Teaching Newer Generations

When I joined IE University as a professor, I thought it was an excellent opportunity, but I did not know that the benefits would far outweigh my expectations.

The subject I taught was Transformational HR, which I loved from the start because transforming the HR function was one of the major drivers of my career. The first year I used a lot of content in my classes. I wanted to impress students with my knowledge, and it went really well. I received a 4.46 evaluation from my students on a scale of 5. I received tons of lessons as a

---

[62] https://www.ie.edu/

professor during that year, but there was an assignment that changed the way I approached the class.

I asked them to prepare an elevator pitch with their own vision of the future for the HR department. I had 28 minds from 20-plus nationalities working on proposals to strengthen the HR department. I was shocked at the results—it was like taking a cover off my eyes. The things they came up with were impressive both for me and for them.

Now, every year I repeat this drill and I get the wonderful gift of learning how newer generations see the future of HR. I am not resistant to the change they are bringing to the workplace. I am looking forward to understanding and supporting their ideas and values.

As I mentioned before, these were the years where I went back to being inspirable and super-connected with my Inspirable Tribe. Many things were happening at the same time.

The Impossible Challenge

In parallel, I was working with a consultancy company on several projects that required change management. I enjoyed it a lot, although sometimes it seemed like we were conducting organizational therapy sessions—which most of them needed—rather than really helping our clients to deliver better results.

One day, we received an interesting request from one of the biggest banks in Europe. They needed a change management program for a 20,000-person subsidiary in Spain to be executed in a three-month period. They also did not want to pay loads of money to an army of consultants.

I remember being in the office and talking with the rest of the team about this "impossible" request. After surrendering to denial, we ended up submitting a traditional proposal with a high price bid, and the potential client immediately said no.

I thought about the situation for weeks. "These kinds of requests are going to be more frequent every year. Whoever finds a solution will hit the jackpot."

The solution was in the air

Later that year, I was attending an HR Tech conference in the U.S., and I needed to change my American Airlines flight from Dallas to Madrid because of a tremendous storm. I thought I was going to wait on the phone for hours, but in less than 15 seconds, a kind but robotic voice spoke to me on the other side. It was the AA customer care chatbot[63]. At that time, except for Amazon's Alexa or Siri, my experiences with chatbots were very frustrating. But this one was fantastic. In two minutes, my flight was changed.

I said to myself, "What if we can create a chatbot for change management and human resources needs?"

Jackpot Time

I was determined to seize the opportunity. I searched for a couple of companies who were willing to test the concept as partners. I got the support of two innovators: Marcos at one of

---

[63] A chatbot it a computer program designed to simulate conversation with human users, especially over the Internet.

the biggest beverage companies in the world and Victoria at an important HR consultancy company.

It was time to deliver, and I started looking for talent to help me design the chatbots.

I met Pedro, who was almost 20 years younger than me. He loved the project and was not interested in making a profit right away. "I just want us to be partners in this," he said. We founded HRbots together, a startup focused on building chatbots to support HR departments and employees.

Pedro and I were from different generations but we worked as equals from the start. We had different strengths: he knew the intricacies of tech and I knew about the use that it could have. We ended up working together on almost everything that was required, like the logo design, the business plan, the potential client database, and, last but not least, enjoying the big parties we had in the WeWork building where HRbots was located.

Three months later, we executed both pilots and gained huge learnings. Later on, Leonor joined the team, and we benefited from her extensive HR experience to create many chatbots. I have to say most of them were for experimental use in areas such as performance management, employee onboarding, outplacement, and transactional services. All this happened thanks to many organizations that supported our project. HRbots won third place for the best HR start-up in Spain in 2019.[64]

---

[64] https://ftransformaespana.es/iv-edicion-talent-summit/

The pandemic took the jackpot away

During the COVID-19 pandemic, all HRbots projects and prospects came to a halt. With uncertainty at its highest and cash reserves depleting, I needed to make a decision: continue pushing for the success of the project or suspend it after three years of joyful (but not profitable) efforts. I decided on the latter one. It was painful, and I have to say that on some long nights during the lockdown I felt I was heading toward square one. But quickly it proved not to be the case; my tribe was there, and I was consciously inspirable.

By the second half of 2020, I had figuratively tattooed my three development areas on my forehead: interesting projects, healthy habits and a joyful life. It turned out to be the most profitable and healthier year of my life, maybe a year too tough to call it joyful, but indeed, the most interesting of all by far.

Be In

Which were the moments when you felt most inspirable in the past five years? Which were the moments when most positive things happened in your life? Any coincidence?

_____

_____

_____

_____

_____

_____

Chapter insights

Being inspirable is about identifying and creating bonds with people who inspire you to grow. It is also about making those bonds stronger every day.

- Some of my strongest bonds were born along a significant project with a disruptive scope like HRbots or the sociometric badges.
- Not only disruptive projects have this effect. I am involved with many people in my tribe in smaller initiatives that could have a reduced impact on our environment, the bond is there, getting stronger. We are permeable to each other.

Actions are a fundamental part of the Inspirable Way©, for the sake of the result and the transformation. Step 4 of the framework, the Inspirable Moves, provides a structure and recommendations to plan your actions.

Chapter 14 - Step 4: The Moves

Are you intentionally involved in actions that foster your growth?

Have you ever run out of willpower because of doing everything on your own?

Would you appreciate extra energy to get involved in interesting stuff?

The personal experiences that I have shared illustrate my journey to become inspirable after a big slump. These are the experiences that enabled me to create this framework for your development. Each of the events I've mentioned ignited one phase of the Inspirable Way©. When I became un-inspirable, I understood I needed to begin an exploration to understand who I wanted to become: my *Inspirable Self*. Then I realized through my coaching experiences that this voyage shouldn't be a lonely one; I needed to be closer to others, belong to a group or a team, then I came up with the idea of the *Inspirable Tribe*. My third finding was about the importance of the context: After founding HRbots in the inspiring WeWork spaces surrounded by exciting people from all over the world, I ended up including the *Inspirable Context*.

In the months after the creation of the framework's initial version, I did tons of research on psychological and sociological documents to support or reject[65] the model. I was happy reaching out to my tribe frequently, which kept me inspired, on the move, exploring. Then I analyzed the conversations I was having with my tribe members, and I identified three types:

1. **Conversations sharing unique experiences.** Everyone in the conversation was sharing something they did and usually the results this was bringing. This type of chat was useful for obtaining fresh concepts from someone who inspired you. For example, in the "health" subject, someone could talk about her experience running, and another person would share his experience fasting. This is good stuff but the downside is that as you have not been through it yourself, it could be too abstract.

2. **Conversations about similar experiences.** I can share two concrete cases: when I talk about teaching with my colleagues at IE University or when I talk with my meditation buddies. Here, the diversity of concepts is less than in the previous type, but the engagement is higher, as facing similar challenges, strengthens the bonds within the group.

3. **Conversations about the same experience together.** This is the one where I have found the highest level of engagement when I got to act in the same initiative along with my tribe fellows. The most recent experience I had related to this point happened while working with a group of people from a company that I have supported for several years in matters related to human development and team cohesion. The team was in charge of reducing the environmental impact of the company. For a few months we met regularly to implement actions such as paper use

---

[65] Some ideas I had did not have any scientific evidence to be used, hence why they are not included in the model.

reduction, increase recycling, and others. In our conversations and actions about how to make this change for the better, we really got the best out of each other, and the outcome for the organization and ourselves was optimum.

These insights paved the way for the fourth step of the method: the Inspirable Moves. Getting involved in activities, initiatives, or projects with people from your Inspirable Tribe will speed up your growth and increase your joy.

It's time to take action

Trying to earn your second degree to expand your career possibilities is a tough thing to do. It's working full time and going to class at night with long hours of study, but if you have a group of classmates who are willing to cheer each other on through many pots of coffee, I'm pretty sure life will seem a lot easier. Without their support, you may give up and drop the class, or you won't get as much knowledge out of it. In my years as a professor, I have seen the difference in learning and grades (which do not always go hand in hand) between the students who work isolated and those who do it connected. Why? Besides the already obvious sharing best practices of having updated information about the course requirements and collaboration to execute complex tasks, they become permeable to the personal traits of their colleagues, such as punctuality, organization, reliability, and others.

Another example is people who work out regularly. Many of them have workout buddies to keep them engaged. When you look at your tribe to pick someone to exercise with, you wouldn't choose someone who hates exercising and is focused on writing his bestselling novel. You'd get together with someone who has a gym membership and enjoys finding different ways to eat healthily. By choosing a tribe member for a specific activity, you're going to grow faster because they will inspire you.

Inverse FOMO

Fear of Missing Out (FOMO) is a syndrome now very common in our society as a consequence of the increased usage of social networks. We want to be everywhere, so while we are spending time with our family, we are chatting with a group of friends on WhatsApp or responding to a long thread or work-related emails.

FOMO usually has a negative connotation as it deprives us of the possibility of enjoying and focusing on the present moment, but you can use FOMO to your advantage. If you join a group that plays tennis every weekend, every time you feel like not going, FOMO will intervene. You will start imagining them having a great time together and improving their skills. This thought will make it tougher for you not to attend. This is the positive perspective of FOMO and one advantage of belonging to tribes.

All you need to do is take action and plan activities together. In a few weeks, your InQ (Inspirable Quotient) will go through the roof. My only recommendation is to be humble here. Getting too ambitious will only create a reference for you that is unreachable, and it will transform into a source of frustration.

This is the thinking of experts in the field like James Clear[66] who says that you should go small, almost atomic-size small. For example, instead of going to the gym three times a week together with your friends, commit to only once a week in the beginning. When going once a week becomes a solid habit, you can increase the number of days. James Clear's main reason for this is that you cannot go big on a habit you have not adopted yet.

You might ask: Do I need to organize activities with my entire tribe? Not at all. You can design your actions to reach groups of different magnitudes. I suggest starting with a duo, just yourself and another person, then you can organize a trio and or a squad. Here are some descriptions and examples of each type.

Group type	Description
Duo	Your actions in a duo are executed by two people, and one of them is yourself. I recommend choosing people from the core of your tribe. I have two duos that have given me significant results when implementing healthy habits for me: 1. Meditation. My friend Peter and I committed to meditating every day and we track it using the app Headspace. 2. My friend Borja and I meet every day at 6:54 am to run to the gym, and neither one of us will break this commitment if it is raining or snowing.
Trio	A trio is a group of three people that will perform one action together. I have an interesting example. My brother, my wife, and I created a trio to improve the execution of our workouts. We never actually workout together, but we can track and cheer each other using the Freeletics app.

---

[66] James Clear. *Atomic Habits: An Easy & Proven Way to Build Good Habits & Break Bad Ones*. (New York: Avery, 2018.)

Squad	A squad is a small group that, according to Jeff Bezos, can be fed with two pizzas. This means fewer than ten people, depending on how hungry everyone is. I was part of a group that for two years met one afternoon a month to talk about personal concerns. We shared the major challenges we were facing in our daily lives and the experiences everyone had when facing similar situations.
Tribe	As previously discussed in the book, Robin Dunbar defined a tribe as a group of a maximum 150 people. But you don't need to worry about including your entire tribe in some kind of activity or meeting. It most likely won't be viable to have actions for all your members for many reasons. Most of them don't know each other or have anything in common besides the fact that they know you. Some of them live in different places around the world. You might only see them in one place if you arrange a grand birthday celebration or at your son's or daughter's wedding (or maybe your own if you're single.) However, don't let this discourage you. Remember, just having identified your Inspirable Tribe and developing your relationships will bring you closer to who you want to become.

Table 5: Action examples per group type

We have talked about the reach you want your actions to have (duos, trios or squads), but what about the role you are going to play in making these actions happen? It depends on your level of comfort. There are three roles you can play:

Figure 14: Three roles to play in tribe activities.

Participate: You only need to say yes to some invitations from your tribe. Taking part is the first step in connecting and generating stronger bonds.

Promote: You are more involved than in the previous step. You will work to have more people taking part in the initiative or keep the current ones engaged. This means communicating, getting people onboard, and sharing the benefits of joining. When you promote initiatives, people will perceive you as someone who wants the best for all involved.

Start: Some people are natural activities organizers for groups since they were young. If this is too intimidating for you, think about the scope involved and maybe you can work it out a little differently. In my case, I don't feel comfortable organizing activities for large groups of people, but I can handle planning for duos, trios, or small squads.

What kinds of activities should you plan or attend?

It depends on the areas you want to develop. Here you have my example of the activities that I took part in, promoted, or created in my tribe according to my development areas:

Interesting projects:

- Research for the Inspirable concept, along with other specialists.
- Mentor MBA students.
- Join a book reading club.

Health initiatives:

- Meditation buddies
- Workout buddies
- I started a well-being community at one company.

Joyful area:

- Join more activities with other parents from school.

There are no limits to the activities you set out to do, just keep two things in mind: first, they should get you closer to the person you would like to become, and second, they should be activities you like and not something to force yourself into. Connecting with others will reduce your need to rely on willpower.

Be In

Name two or three actions that you would like to do with some people in your tribe. Define the arrangement: duo, trio, or squad and the role you are going to play: creator, promoter, or participant?

_____

_____

_____

_____

_____

_____

_____

_____

Less willpower, more joy needed

The fundamental challenge to growing is our resistance to change. Our energy is there, waiting to be unleashed. Until now, you have been using your willpower every time you wanted to change something in your life. The problem—willpower—is finite, and when you are out of it, you go back to previous behaviors. The solution is to reduce the willpower spent in every transformation.

 If you have gotten this far, and you have been practicing the cycle steps, you know by now the secret formula of this approach:

$$Willpower\ needed = \frac{Your\ full\ willpower}{No.\ of\ people\ involved}$$

Let me show you one example. Suppose you want to become a more inclusive leader. If your full willpower (wp) is 100 wp units and you don't involve anyone from your tribe to join you in this learning path, your equation will have the following result:

$$Willpower\ needed = \frac{Your\ full\ willpower\ (100)}{No.\ of\ people\ involved(1)} = 100wp$$

Meaning, you will deplete all your willpower resources. If you decide to involve your boss and one of your peers so that you can all together become better leaders, such as sharing content and giving each other feedback, then your equation will look like this:

$$Willpower\ needed = \frac{Your\ full\ willpower\ (100)}{No.\ of\ people\ involved(3)} = 33wp$$

Not only will you use less willpower to achieve your transformation, but you will have plenty of wp to use it for other purposes:

Wp available = Full Wp (100) − Wp needed (33) = 67 wp

Of course, this is a hypothetical calculation. There is no such a thing as "wp units," but I'm sure that after a few runs, you will agree with its fundamentals. The reason behind these formulas is clear: Involving positive people in your development increases your joy. *You do it because you want to, not because you have to.*

The way of life

As you use these steps throughout your life, some cycles will be more intensive while others will be easier. It's about constant self-improvement: the more you do it, the more insights you will receive and the better you will get.

After a few runs, the Inspirable Way© will become your way of life. Is there a better habit than the one that makes you a better person every day? I doubt it.

Chapter Insights

When you identify your Inspirable Self and Inspirable Tribe, your self-confidence gets an immediate boost. "If these are the people I'm connected to, I will succeed."

Then you start tweaking your Inspirable Context to make sure your brain is getting the right messages all the time. Reducing the friction of the change you want to implement makes the journey even smoother.

Still, your tribe, the people that you have selected from the many tribes you belong to, continues to move organically, without your direct intervention, until now.

With the Inspirable Moves step, you have realized that if you take an active role (participating, promoting or creating initiatives) in your tribe, then boom! Engagement will go through the roof, the bond will get stronger, and connections among people that did not exist before your involvement now will play an important role in inspiring everyone.

Chapter 15 - Step 5: The Gains

Are you frustrated because of measuring yourself against ideals?

When was the last time you celebrated an achievement?

How long did the sense of achievement last?

When you want to achieve something very concrete, setting a goal and measuring your progress against it is good practice. If you want to write a book, you could define a goal of the number of pages you need to write every week. If you want to run a marathon, you'll need to specify the distance you are going to be running every day to complete it successfully.

However, this approach is not adequate if you want to transform as a person and enhance your well-being. If you're focused just on what you want to achieve, you miss out on the exploration, the process, the journey. Being open to experience is the way you're going to find your better self.

That's why I'm not talking about goals, timelines, and deadlines in this book. These are useful as guidelines and references, but as a person focused on my development, if I use a goal-focused approach, I'm going to get frustrated. It'll feel like I'm working for others and not for myself.

Another reason it doesn't make sense to set concrete goals when related to personal development is because it is uncharted territory. If you have never done it before, then how can you be so sure you will get there, or that you will want to get there once you start the journey?

Focus on the gains, not on the goals

To measure progress, you can use the concept of *gain*, which I got from *The Gap and the Gain* by Dan Sullivan and Benjamin Hardy.

Sullivan, one of the most experienced corporate coaches in the world, says that "The way to measure your progress is backward against where you started, not against your ideal."[67]

A gain is something you did not have before today, such as a new skill, a project, a relationship, getting closer to a person, a new habit, or even getting rid of an old habit. Thinking about your gains will make you stop thinking about the gap. The gap is the difference between your current situation with an unattainable goal or ideal.

I encourage you to measure success in comparison with yourself yesterday, the month before, or the year before. The answer to the question: What have I gained? It could be simply "I learned how to cook pad thai" or something that takes longer, such as "I made my first corporate presentation in French." It could even be something material, such as buying your first

---

[67] Sullivan and Dr Benjamin Hardy. *The Gap and The Gain: The High Achievers' Guide to Happiness, Confidence, and Success*. (Carlsbad, CA: Hay House Business, 2021.)

home or a new sofa. In the past, you did not have it and now you do, so it is something to be proud of.

Using goals and deadlines frequently brings stress and depletes your willpower. The syndrome of *The Hedonic Treadmill* defined by Michael Eysenck[68] describes a behavior where:

- You achieve a goal, like getting promoted.
- You get used to your new situation.
- You become unsatisfied again.

Focusing on the gains guarantees you avoid the treadmill dip; instead, you will stay positive, looking at your accomplishments every day.

Types of Gains

Gain types can be infinite if you have a creative mind. The more you can identify, the better, because it will keep your mind focused on the positives of your journey. Thinking about the productive, vitality and transformational[69] assets that Gratton and Scott mention in Chapter 7 as key to a 100-year life, I made a list of the most common gains people usually identify:

Skills. This includes learning something new, like understanding a new culture, understanding the basics of

---

[68] Seph Fontane Pennock. The Hedonic Treadmill – Are We Forever Chasing Rainbows?" *Positive Psychology*. Sept. 5, 2016.
https://positivepsychology.com/hedonic-treadmill/
[69] Productive assets are those that help individuals become valuable and therefore boost their income.
Vitality assets are those practices that bring physical and mental health. Transformation assets are those that help us go through life's transitions.

coding, getting familiar with agile methodologies, or designing your own clothes.

Property. You have been able to purchase something you need or want, such as a new home, a car, a book, or clothing. This might sound materialistic, but there is nothing to be ashamed about here. If you got it, celebrate it.

Relations. Maybe you met someone interesting, or you solved a conflict in your work. It could also be that you had a team-building experience with your colleagues. In your family circle, it could have been a great conversation with your parents or a nice dinner with your spouse.

Habits. This is very interesting because it is not every day that we incorporate a new habit or kick an old one, but if we are aware, we will notice tiny improvements: We are sleeping better, running faster, or becoming more organized at work.

Mindset. For me, this is one of the most difficult to spot. How do we notice that our mindset has changed? Although this is not that simple, when I face a difficult situation, I ask myself, how would I have handled this in the past? I do these comparisons using longer-term periods, such as one year ago or 10 years ago. Try it. You are going to be surprised with your answers. An example of gains in this area is when you realize you are listening more to your children or you are having more productive reactions each time a new problem arises.

Two actions to measure your gains

There are some days when it won't be easy to identify your gains. Maybe things did not go well at all; you might be tired. These two actions will make it easier for you:

First, **be grateful.** It's simply asking yourself what you have that you didn't have a day ago, a week ago, etc. Every time you do it, it's a great opportunity to be thankful for your gains. This is very easy and can be done daily.

Second, **be reflective.** After you have to respond to the question of the grateful approach, then you ask yourself: *Which people in your tribe contributed most to those gains?* Make sure you have your tribe chart with you to identify who you need to bring closer to the inner core.

If you have doubts about whom to bring closer, there is a great exercise to assess the value of people's contributions proposed by Dr. Hardy: Imagine that you never met that person you are thinking of. What would you lose in your life with this hypothetical alternative?

You can use the grateful approach on a weekly basis or even daily. I recommend using the reflective approach at least once a month.

The last of the five-step cycle

With the measuring of the gains, we conclude the five-step cycle of the Inspirable Way©. It is meant to be a sequence. Every step comes after the previous one. The five steps are there to guide you, but your situation will define the time you need to spend in each step.

I have seen a big variation in the time people take to complete the cycle of five steps, depending on the person and their circumstances. I can also say that it is very common that people take around one or two months to complete the first cycle, but then there are cycles that some finish in a few days.

After you measure your gains, you will move again to Step One: The Inspirable Self and begin another cycle through validating if the two, three or four areas you have identified for growth are the ones you want to keep, or if you need to make any changes. Why? Because we need to make sure this vision is always up-to-date. In some cycles we will not touch it and in some we will make big changes to it.

Be In

Which gains have you obtained during the past month? Who contributed the most to these gains?

_____

_____

_____

_____

_____

_____

_____

Chapter Insights

Being inspired by others brings excitement and growth to your life, but comparing yourself to others only brings fear and frustration.

It is natural that companies set goals and milestones to make sure that everyone works together toward that target. It is also a good idea to set some goals for yourself when you want to achieve concrete stuff like learning to dance salsa or running a marathon. This makes sense because what you are trying to achieve has been done before by others. Countless companies try to sell their products and services every day. Hundreds of thousands of individuals are getting ready for their first marathon while you are reading this book; however:

- When you want to address broader personal areas like becoming a better leader, having a healthier life, or being a better parent, this is a unique journey. You might have access to similar experiences and could have tried it before, but you have different circumstances each day.
- This is the reason this journey is not to take you from A to B, but for exploration. So, you will not measure yourself against what others have achieved. You will only compare yourself with the person you were in the past. This could be yesterday or 10 years ago. *What do you have now that you did not have back then?* It could be a skill, a property, or a habit.
- Every time you feel your joy is fading, start listing your gains and you will see the excitement flowing immediately.

PART III - INSPIRABLE FUTURE

Chapter 16 - Inspirable Organizations

How do you build an Inspirable Organization (IO)?

Which are the fundamental differences between an IO and a traditional one?

How do you measure an organization's InQ?

The individual who most contributed to Jane's growth during the last year is Mike, who works right next to her. But he has not been the person who has taught her more stuff or even supported her the most with solving work-related problems. He is not working directly with her, and, as a matter of fact, the work they do is completely unrelated. Then, how can their relationship be so productive?

If you dig deeper, you can find some clues to this enigma.

- They get along pretty well, usually go for coffee together and engage in small talk while they work.
- They are very different. Jane is 20 years older than Mike and they were born in different continents. However, she has developed a genuine interest in him and likewise.
- Their jobs are very different. Jane works in corporate communications and Mike is an executive assistant. Working close to him, she has improved her organization

skills big time, and also imitates the way he interacts with others, which has made her kinder.

Jane had a conversation with her manager who recognized that she has become more effective at work and building better relationships with her colleagues. She was becoming a strong candidate for leading one of the key projects for the company. At home, her spouse has praised her for how much she has changed and how this has improved their relationship in the past few months.

Mike has signed up for a master's degree program in corporate communications, as he has understood the strategic value of this function after many conversations with Jane and, most importantly, she has inspired him to continue to grow his career.

What you see here is the typical case of an employee becoming inspirable. All consequences are positive for the people involved, their surrounding group, and even for the organizational results. Yet, most of the time, these events happen unnoticed in businesses. This is because *most organizations focus on narrow short-term goals, even regarding people's development.*

We have discussed similar situations throughout the book most of the time from the perspective of the individual, but from the organizational viewpoint we need to stop and think, or better yet, dream:

What would a company where most of its members are inspirable look like?

What you are about to read is a theoretical extrapolation of my work with inspirable individuals and the effect that I predict will have on any organization. Some aspects of this proposal might seem futuristic, but there are many companies already taking steps toward models that allow them to seize the opportunities the future environment will bring. I'm going to share with you how to understand the Inspirable Organization, visualize it, its key principles, how to make its progress, and how to measure its progress.

How to visualize an Inspirable Organization

The main differentiator of an inspirable organization (IO) in comparison with a regular one, is the possibility of its members to create strong bonds among people in ways not necessarily pre-determined by its board of directors. For this reason, an IO cannot be represented using an organizational chart. It doesn't mean you have to ditch it; you might still need it for certain governance purposes.

An IO is more like a network, but we need to avoid considering the inspirable organization as a networking place. People connected in a traditional network are usually looking to achieve a goal through each connection, whereas the purpose of the people that are part of an inspirable organization is to become better individuals in many aspects of life. This means that the bonds created in these groups usually transcend the groups.

So, the most appropriate way to represent it is using a network map, also called a sociogram. The following network map displays a team that could belong to a hypothetical organization. The circles represent the people in the team and the lines connect people who interact frequently.

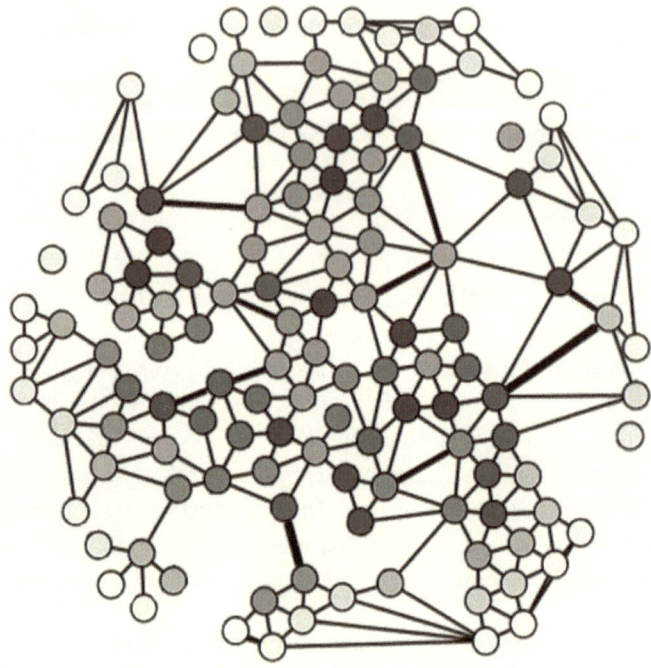

Figure 15: Network map or Sociogram. Image author: Claudio Rocchini, modified by Daniel Laya.

How to build your network map

A network map or sociogram is a tool within the social science discipline of sociometry, a quantitative method for measuring social relationships developed by psychotherapist Jacob L. Moreno[70] along with social psychologist Helen Hall Jennings[71] during the 1950s. Social network analysis has evolved amazingly since then. If you are interested in knowing more about it, I recommend you check out authors like Charles

---

[70] "Jacob L. Moreno." *Wikipedia.* April 15, 2022.
https://en.wikipedia.org/wiki/Jacob_L._Moreno
[71] "Helen Hall Jennings." Wikipedia. July 10, 2022.
https://en.wikipedia.org/wiki/Helen_Hall_Jennings

Kadushin[72], Alex Pentland[73], and, from a more organizational perspective, Ben Waber[74].

You can build a network map to study almost any behavioral variable in the organization, such as leadership, influence, collaboration, cohesion, or, in our case, the permeability to other's positive behavior, meaning, being inspirable.

The easy way to build an inspirable network map for your organization is to do a survey to ask everyone in the team, department, or organization two questions:

1. Mention the names of the people within the team or organization that you think are more permeable to the positive behaviors of others (Inspirable people). These are people that frequently incorporate best practices and positive habits from colleagues, listen to others' advice, and get inspired or amazed by others. Score the magnitude of the *inspirable* level of each person, 10 being the maximum inspiration and 1 the minimum.
2. Mention the names of five people within the team or organization who have inspired you the most in the past 6 months (Inspirational people). Score the magnitude of the *inspirational* level of each person, 10 being the maximum inspiration and 1 the minimum.

[72] Charles Kadushin. *Understanding Social Networks: Theories, Concepts, and Findings.* (Oxford University Press: New York, 2011.)

[73] Alex Pentland. *Social Physics: How Social Networks Can Make Us Smarter.* (Penguin Books: New York, NY, 2015.)

[74] Ben Waber. *People Analytics: How Social Sensing Technology Will Transform Business and What It Tells Us about the Future of Work.* (Pearson: London, 2013.)

With this information, you can use one of the many apps available[75] in the market to create your network map.

How to interpret the network map

The map with this information will show who is inspirable and how they are connected by links in the sociogram. It will also show you who are the most inspirable people in the organization: those who have the highest number of links leading to them. Here, it is also important to take into consideration the magnitude of the link, which will be represented in the link's thickness in the network map.

The most common reasons people show connected on this network map are:

- The obvious one: *they work with each other* and they need to coordinate constantly. This constant communication and the openness of each person has made them inspirable by each other.
- *They are physically close to each other*, maybe even sitting next to each other, so they interact even if they don't work together. Having the opportunity to communicate frequently increases the odds of being inspirable by the other person.
- *They like each other*, they enjoy their company, so they are constantly asking each other for advice on work or non-work issues.

---

[75] Kumar, Varun. "23 Free Social Network Analysis Tools [As of 2022]." *RankRed*. January 3, 2022. https://www.rankred.com/free-social-network-analysis-tools/

Also, keep in mind it is very common to find people who do not show connection on the sociogram, the most frequent reasons are:

- They don't work with each other.
- They do work together but don't get along well, so they keep their communication to a minimum.
- Although they belong to the same department, they work on different shifts or locations.

Calculating your Organization's Inspirable Quotient

You can make the calculation as precise as you want, using a worksheet to calculate first the Inspirable Quotient for each individual:

$Indiv. InQ = No. of links to the individual \times Avg link thickness$

Once you have it, you can calculate the Organizational Inspirable Quotient:

$Organizational InQ = Avg of all Individual InQ$

The Organizational InQ will enable you to track the evolution of your organization to become a more inspirable one by doing a survey or pulse check many times a year.

It is important to highlight that, in this kind of analysis, the visuals tell you more than the numbers. Which areas of your team are isolated? Who is connecting with most people? What is the nature of the activity that connects them? Is it personal and/or professional?

The most important question to ask your sociogram is this: To what degree are people bonding in your organization?

It's all about bonding

An inspirable organization is about bonding. It is not about connecting everybody, but it is about *giving everybody the opportunity to bond*. If you create an environment where inspirable people can be closer together (physically or virtually), they will start inspiring each other and the organization will develop organically.

Now, regardless of the way the inspirable organization is formed, you will need to create an environment that allows it to blossom. There is a common set of principles that will make this happen.

The Inspirable Organization principles

Any organization can become an inspirable one. The inspirable principles should work in most organizational types. From organizations with traditional authority-led cultures to the value-driven ones, these are the three principles that will facilitate its members to be inspirable.

Openness. People in an inspirable workplace need to have an open mind and heart for sharing and receiving. This means that people are always trying to reach out to other colleagues for advice, for support, because they care about their well-being.

They are also receptive to feedback, advice, and, of course, inspiration.

Safeness. The workplace needs to be psychologically safe. People should be able to bring their entire selves to work, and they will do it only if they don't feel threatened. Employees have to feel is entirely safe to connect with everyone regardless of paygrade, gender, political views, race, sexual orientation, physical ability, ethnicity, or age. Individuals who feel safe will start actions to strengthen their bonds.

Well-being. People should care and act to keep at the highest level possible the physical and mental health of everyone in the organization. This includes creating an environment that reduces stress and contributes to peace of mind. A higher level of well-being will bring better results, higher employee and client retention, and a wider and deeper impact on society.

The level of presence of these principles will vary in each organization. No matter what level each value is in a specific organization, it can always do better. For example, you might find a business with a medium level of openness, where most of its staff are always collaborating, but it still can grow if people start sharing what makes them tick in life, what their priorities are for development or what kind of person they want to become.

Tangible differences with the traditional organization

As the Inspirable Principles gain traction within an organization, there will be many changes happening within it. Some departments will set new priorities, and many behaviors will change. Here are the most common variations you will see:

The role of the Inspirable Story. Stories are a powerful way to connect people, and people in an Inspirable Organization will become good at storytelling, especially when it comes to tell stories about their gains, who contributed to them, and which benefits this brought to all those around them. Stories are the main reinforcers of the new culture arising.

Talent acquisition. HR professionals are always in conversations with potential candidates to join the organization. The primary source of talent comes from employee referrals. The recruitment conversation differs completely from the regular interview. Here, the role of the HR person is to be a role model of the inspirable principles. She needs to show openness, create a safe environment, and share the way the organization cares about the well-being of the employees. The HR person also acts as a coach, helping the candidate build his own inspirable story. It is common for a candidate to be invited to the office for coffee or lunch with other groups not related to the department they could be joining, creating the bonds that start well before the official process.

People development. People have ownership of their own development. In this scenario, the dream of the HR people and CEO has come true. It is important for HR departments to understand that they cannot establish the direction of development. They can provide guidance and advice, but the employees are the ones who decide their growth. Once the individual decides, the HR person can give visibility of who at the organization has those strengths, and even introduce them to each other.

Talent retention. Salary, perks, retention bonuses, stock options, and a company car are secondary. They just need to be in line with what the labor market offers, but it is not a tool for retention. People stay in the inspirable organization because this is the place where they grow every day, even beyond the organization's needs.

The way employees sell and relate to clients. For an inspirable salesperson, key account manager or customer care representative, each contact with the client is not a burden but an opportunity. Customers are part of their inspirable tribe. Salespeople might have sales goals to reach and customer satisfaction levels to maintain, but this is not their chief concern; it is building the best relation possible with their clients. This way, they both grow as individuals while impacting the bottom line of their businesses.

Innovation. As a result, of the previous point, by having a sales force or a customer care team that frequently gets inspired by their clients, there is a lot of honest feedback about the company's product and services coming from them. As the product development department gets thrilled ever' time they have conversations with the sales and customer care team, they are eager to transform this feedback into product and service improvements. This honest relationship along the value chain frequently creates innovations that the competitors cannot immediately replicate.

Working space. This space has to encourage reaching out and connecting easily with those around you for the important things, as well as the tiny things. Most of us work in hybrid spaces. Sometimes we are sharing the physical space with our colleagues, and sometimes we are sharing a virtual space. We need to take both into consideration.

The physical space. In year 2009, MIT's media lab research group developed innovative methods for examining the impact of workplace socializing. Using specially designed badges embedded with a radio transceiver, a microphone, a microprocessor, and a set of motion sensors, they could track and record information such as the wearer's location, direction, and voice inflections. From this research, MIT's startup Humanyze was born, and years later they allowed our company mIDentity to use this technology in Spain.

One of the most interesting discoveries was the "water cooler effect". For a few months, every employee of a call center wore one of those devices during working hours. After analyzing the data, they discovered that the most productive conversations did not happen in meeting rooms but around the water coolers. Coffee machines, printers, watercoolers and similar meeting places are where informal conversations about tacit knowledge, shared attitudes, work habits, and how to manage specific situations, people, and problems take place. With its research, Humanyze discovered not only that the cohesion of the team increased but also that overall productivity increased from 10 to 15%.[76]

When working spaces are designed, it is very common to dedicate a lot of time to thinking where each employee is going to have their place to work, and also the number and sizes of the meeting rooms. Informal meeting places are usually overlooked because most managers still consider informal interaction as nonproductive, but for an inspirable organization, informal interaction is everything.

The virtual space. When we are connected to our organization through collaborative videoconferencing, chat platforms, or using virtual reality devices, in theory connecting with anyone should be instantaneous. You just need to press the button and the call will start. However, we are frequently inhibited from doing it. What if that person is busy? Maybe I'm calling too often, I should email instead, I don't like to be stuck on the

---

[76] Alex Pentland. "The Water Cooler Effect." *Psychology Today.* Nov. 22, 2009. https://www.psychologytoday.com/intl/blog/reality-mining/200911/the-water-cooler-effect

screen all the time. Frustration is a recurrent feeling in the virtual world. Even if, for some of us, most of our work is happening in the virtual space, we are still in the early stages of the learning curve. An average senior manager spent the first 20 years of her career without videoconferencing, so it is understandable that after two or three years of doing it, they are still not experts.

The solution is part technical and part human. For the first section, some organizations might need to include collaboration technologies that go beyond Slack or Teams and simulate working environments. One example of this is Gather[77], which includes the usual perks that platforms like Zoom, Google Meet, Teams or Slack have, but on top of this, it provides a visual of your virtual environment. In this virtual office, every member of the organization has an avatar that can move around and interact with other people. The interesting part is that if you need some privacy for a conversation, you can "walk" to a meeting room with the person you want to talk to without interruptions, as the rest will see that both of you are having a meeting. This is the same way you can enter your boss's office because you see there is nobody else in there and she is not on a call or marked with a busy status. As technology and company culture evolve, hybrid environments will become great connection hubs.

Gather is just one alternative. By the time I write this, tens of start-ups[78] are also launching their platforms to be the best option to connect people in hybrid spaces, including the development of Metaverse, Mark Zuckerberg's virtual world proposal.

---

[77] https://www.gather.town/
[78] Recent options are Teamflow (https://www.teamflowhq.com/) and Cosmos video (https://cosmos.video/).

Get professional support

Growing small and even medium organizations to become IOs should not be a difficult task, as long as most of its members behave according to the IO principles. Certainly this involves many complexities when you want to do the same in a large multinational. To do it in a reasonable period, you'll need technology and a support team that can act globally. There are already options that can cover both.

Haider Imam co-founded TAO Leadership[79] with the purpose of providing a scientific understanding of how tribes connect and impact on the business results. The company created software that analyzes all the connections within an organization no matter the number of employees, and also designed the diagnose framework to understand the key problems detected.

Its solution was especially good at detecting the change agents, those informal influencers within the organizations. These change agents are the people who can drive change and create a tipping point for successful transformation, who help workers do their jobs better or just have a good pulse of the company morale.

Remarkably, it found that in most of the cases, these key influencers were not at the highest levels of the organizational chart, and in some organizations, they did not have a single influencer in the top management team. For decades,

---

[79] In year 2021, the global consulting firm EY acquired TAO Leadership, expanding its scope to a different level, which is now able to work with organizations with hundreds of thousands of employees. I'm eager to hear about their new findings in organizational behavior to improve workplaces worldwide.

organizational change was driven top down. No wonder it has such a high failure rate!

With this scenario, the TAO Leadership team developed an agile framework to address the improvements needed in each client company, not disregarding the importance of having top management engaged but additionally focusing on the power of the influencers to bring solutions and implement them. In time, it was easy for them to demonstrate that this approach had superior effectiveness in terms of culture transformation and revenue growth.

When I heard about the "informal influencer" approach, I thought to myself, there has to be a direct relation between the number of influencers in an organization and the number of people inspirable. An organization cannot have influencers if nobody is permeable to them.

The condition of being an influencer doesn't exclude the condition of being inspirable; it is the other way around. I think all influencers are inspirable, as non-inspirable pseudo-influencers are just directors. Also, not everyone inspirable is an influencer, as the person might lack some conditions needed for being a change agent.

After being in contact with many ways to achieve the cultural change needed to become an IO, I think that Haider's TAO Leadership has an interesting combination of technology, global coverage, and flexibility to help large organizations to become inspirable. I'm sure other firms will follow suit, as we are witnessing the dawn of a new kind of organization.

What about leadership?

The role of the leader and anyone else who is responsible for teams is very important to help the organization become more inspirable every day.

Brené Brown talked about vulnerability long ago in her famous TED Talk video[80], the leader who inspires others is the leader who is vulnerable. A leader is not perfect or invincible. He must be vulnerable and share his own personal stories of strengths and weaknesses with the team. He should share his own needs while considering what others need for themselves, in terms of growth and support. A vulnerable leader is not by necessarily an Inspirable Leader, but *a leader that is not vulnerable cannot be inspirable*. So, the first is a requisite.

An Inspirable Organization requires an Inspirable Leader, and that leader needs to avoid being the single source of inspiration at all costs. The leader has to guarantee that the environment fosters the growth of many people as sources of inspiration and facilitates positive bonding.

The leader has to be a coach. The transition from a traditional organization to an inspirable one is full of doubts and contradictions, so the person in charge has to support them with powerful coaching skills, such as empathic listening and questioning.

The person leading an IO should be constantly taking the pulse of the organization, making sure the values are in place, and the organizational design and processes support the values.

---

[80] Brené Brown. "The power of vulnerability." TEDxHouston. December 2010. https://www.ted.com/talks/brene_brown_the_power_of_vulnerability?language=en

The leader's major responsibility is to be a role model, acting according to the three principles all the time: openness, safeness and well-being. The embedding of the principles is mainly a leadership responsibility; they have to do it through constant communication of gains stories. The leader has to walk the talk. At an inspirable organization, the leader's behaviors must be a source of inspiration for others.

There is one question the leader has to ask himself every working day: Is this organization more inspirable than yesterday?

Chapter Insights

An inspirable organization is one where most, if not all its members are permeable to the positive behaviors of others. For this to happen:

- Three principles must be widely shared: openness, safeness and well-being. To grow, the IO has to attract and develop people who have those principles embedded.
- The principles of the IO will shape many areas of the business, such as: talent acquisition and development, onboarding, customer relations, and innovation. It will also shape the way physical and virtual environments are structured.
- There is a body of work that needs to develop further, that is about analyzing inspirable organizations, how to score their levels of evolution, and what important roles like the change agent need to be monitored. In the next few years, a wide variety of approaches will become available to make it happen.

- There are many traits an Inspirable Leader should have: vulnerability and a good coach and manager, but the most important, be the role model of the IO principles and check the pulse every day on how the organization is doing on those.

Chapter 17 - Building an Inspirable Society

What's the use of the Inspirable Way© in a polarized society?

Are solutions for polarization just around the corner?

How can we all contribute to building Inspirable Communities?

Writing about a subject such as being inspirable has changed my view of the world around me.

Initially, I focused on the individual and its potential to grow, creating meaningful connections with others, but as I continued writing, I started thinking: If using the Inspirable Way© has been so positive for me and for those around me, I need to replicate it in organizations. This is the reason I dedicated the final chapters of this book to this subject, expecting to generate curiosity in some business leaders that could get excited about building an inspirable team and then expanding the initiative's impact on our society.

However, by the time I finished my first manuscript, another dark episode of humankind's story started with Russia invading

Ukraine. People were fleeing their homes, their country. NATO imposing sanctions; the word nuclear was again on the news every day.

I felt frustrated to realize we were still living in the world of east and west, left and right, conservatives and liberal, women and men, right and wrong. In the '90s, the word globalization inspired me, but now our world seems more divided than a global community.

But what if?

What if we lived in a world where instead of disconnecting because of fear, we connect looking for inspiration? If we can create a vaccine in months instead of years for the good of humanity, it means there is a special power in humankind that needs to be unleashed.

From my limited understanding of how our world works, but because of the type of content I am most interested in, I think there are three changes that can contribute to create the context for an Inspirable Society to flourish: we need to upgrade our brain, change the algorithm, and become better citizens.

Upgrade our Brain

According to psychologist and Nobel award-winning Daniel Kahneman, author of the bestselling *Thinking, Fast and Slow*[81], we have two ways of making decisions: the intuitive aka the **fast** one, and the rational aka the **slow** one. The speed difference is related to the area of the brain that intervenes in each of them. The fastest way is there to protect us from external dangers

---

[81] Daniel Kahneman. *Thinking, Fast and Slow*. (London: Farrar, Straus and Giroux, 2011.)

where we need to fight, freeze, or flee. This system activates when there is a lion coming toward us or when a man from the neighboring village comes to attack us with an axe.

Most of these types of threats are very infrequent in our modern times where lions are usually very far from us, or sadly, locked in cages. Also, in most countries, people walking with an axe in hand will be stopped by the police every 100 meters.

The problem with the brain's fast system in our current times is that it activates in reaction to simple external events such as having a conflict with your boss like if a lion is coming towards you, or when arguing with your spouse who will pick up the children from school today like the same lion is about to bite you. It is the first cause of our overreactions.

A society of overreacting people turns into a polarized society. The concerns about polarization is not new. Polish social-psychologist Henri Tajfel, after several many experiments in groups during the '60s, came to the following conclusion:

"

"The most important principle of the subjective social order we construct for ourselves is the classification of groups as 'we' and 'they', and once someone becomes a 'they' we are used to dismissing them, competing against them, discriminating against them. Even if there is no reason for it in terms of our own interests."[82]

---

[82] Tajfel, Henri. 'Experiments in Intergroup Discrimination'. Scientific American 223, no. 5 (November 1970): 96–102. https://doi.org/10.1038/scientificamerican1170-96

This means it is going to be very difficult to change it without modulating our brain and helping it adapt to our day and age. Will this upgrade come as hardware like implants, cyborg style, or software through DOSE[83] pills (dopamine, oxytocin, serotonin, and endorphins) that regulate our mental activity? I don't know the answer to this, but it seems unlikely that we can re-educate 8 billion people with mindfulness and meditation. For the record, mindfulness and meditation would be my preferred approach.

Change the Algorithm

Since the invention of the landline phone until the first decade of the 21st century, technology connected humanity worldwide, becoming the cornerstone of globalization. However, with the use and abuse of smartphones and social networks, this started turning in the opposite direction, separating us from each other.

Facebook incorporated its famous EdgeRank[84] content algorithms in 2007. In the beginning, its purpose was to provide content more relevant to the users and increase their satisfaction. Later, other social networks like Instagram and Twitter followed suit.

Quickly, the platforms realized that the most polarized content generated the highest engagement, thus generating more

---

[83] In simplistic terms: Dopamine is the hormone that motivates us to achieve a reward; oxytocin is the "love hormone" responsible for our feelings of attraction and bonding; serotonin regulates our mood (happiness to depression), appetite and digestion; and endorphins reduce pain and increase pleasure. "Get Your Daily DOSE of Happiness." *Cambridge Network*. Jan. 13, 2021. https://www.cambridgenetwork.co.uk/news/get-your-daily-dose-happiness

[84] Matt McGee. "EdgeRank Is Dead: Facebook's News Feed Algorithm Now Has Close To 100K Weight Factors." *Martech*. Aug. 16, 2013. https://martech.org/edgerank-is-dead-facebooks-news-feed-algorithm-now-has-close-to-100k-weight-factors/

revenue and hateful content. Having billions of people connected to social networks absorbing fake polarizing media accelerated the division in our societies for the sake of more money.

Until now, private companies have decided and designed social network algorithms. Because of the consequences our societies are facing, in the near future, some of these decisions will need to abide by standards set by regulations like the Digital Services Act[85], currently in discussion by the European Commission.

Social networks have proven to be precious, but the algorithm needs to favor connection, not division. Hopefully future algorithms will encourage bonding and people development, planting the seeds of an Inspirable Society.

Become better citizens

In this third aspect, I will place a special responsibility on myself and you. In comparison with the rest of the people in our societies, we are privileged in terms of wealth, education, and, I dare to say, even to love and be loved.

While we wait for our brains to be upgraded, for the algorithm to improve, and our leaders to step up to the challenge, we need to act immediately on two fronts:

1. **Ourselves**. We have the right and the duty to become healthier, to grow personally and professionally, and to foster our peace of mind.

---

[85] "Proposal for a regulation of the European Parliament and of the Council on a single market for digital services (digital services act) and amending Directive 2000/31/EC." Commission 2019-24. European Parliament. https://www.europarl.europa.eu/legislative-train/theme-a-europe-fit-for-the-digital-age/file-digital-services-act

2. **With others**. We need to become role models of kindness, empathy, balance, and ethics. We must grow to be beacons in our Inspirable Tribes. Our duty is to act as connectors, leaving no one behind.

This is not a task or a project; it is a way of life. For change to begin and an Inspirable Society to form, it begins with you and me. We just need to stay inspirable.

Welcome to the tribe.

APPENDIX

Appendix A - Stories of Inspirable People

As I mentioned in the introduction, I had four primary sources of inspiration that allowed me to write this book; my personal journey, my professional journey, my research, and the stories of others.

Since I thought for the first time about the Inspirable concept and its importance for our development and adaptation, I started looking for inspirable people around me every day. I found that identifying people through observation only is quite tricky because you need to observe how that person behaves for a decent amount of time to have a proper sample and to check if that person is inspirable most of the time or only had an inspirable burst. So, I moved into a proactive approach and started interviewing people in my circles who I thought to be inspirable. I used some variations of the questions from the Inspirable Quotient questionnaire. The result provided me with a deeper knowledge of what it meant to be inspirable, and who had the skill and who didn't.

Then I analyzed the biographies, conferences, and interviews of dozens of public personalities so that I could share some tangible, inspirable examples with you. Here are four that are top on my list.

Rafael Nadal: Tennis player

Rafael Nadal is a Spanish professional tennis player born in Manacor (Mallorca) in the year 1986. During his career he has been ranked as the world's No. 1 player for more than 200 weeks by the Association of Tennis Professionals (ATP). By the time of the writing of this book, Rafael has won 22 Grand Slam men's single titles[86], including a record 14 French Open titles. This has earned him the nickname "The King of Clay" because of his domination of the clay courts tournaments.

Since I moved to Spain in 2010, I have witnessed the big value that Rafa has for everyone in the country because of his achievements, his temper, and, maybe most importantly, his values and how he got there by staying true to himself.

Tennis is a very individual game where ego can go through the roof if you are not careful, but two elements made me think of Nadal as an inspirable person.

First, he was born inspirable, within a family that could recognize his talent and provide an environment where he could take it to its highest level. He had a very close relationship with Toni Nadal[87], his uncle and coach for 17 years. As most relationships between a high-performance athlete and a high-demanding coach, it was not always on good terms, but as Toni says, Rafael absorbed the most important: Having a never-surrender attitude and keeping his brain active.

Carlos Moyá, the former World No.1 tennis player, was Toni Nadal's successor as Rafael's coach since 2016. Carlos and

---

[86] "Rafael Nadal" *Wikipedia*. Accessed July 21, 2022. https://en.wikipedia.org/wiki/Rafael_Nadal

[87] Jonathan Jurejko. "Rafael Nadal: El tío Toni, el entrenador 'inflexible' y generoso que convirtió a Nadal en uno de los mejores tenistas de la historia." *BBC News Mundo*. January 31, 2022. https://www.bbc.com/mundo/deportes-60193624

Rafa have been friends since their childhood, which is evidence of an inspirable pattern in Rafael: He keeps the inner core of his tribe strong and it is the major source of inspiration for his decisions. Carlos says that Rafa always keeps his ego under control, constantly listening to the team's recommendations humbly[88]. This behavior represents the "beginner's mind" or shoshin, which is so important to being inspirable.

One thing that reassured me the most to think of Rafael Nadal as an inspirable person is his relationship with his rivals, especially with his arch-rival Roger Federer[89].

I have been a tennis fan since the time of the rivalries of Jimmy Connors and Ivan Lendl, and later with Pete Sampras vs. Andre Agassi. Even if I have always been used the importance of respect and proper manners on the tennis court, I have always loved the gentleman behavior that both Nadal and Federer exhibited during every match, and how this has transformed over the years into a friendship relationship and a big source of inspiration for both.

Nadal prides himself on the intensity of his game, but he admits being inspired by the elegance of his counterpart Federer. Federer thinks that although they seem to play with a completely different approach, "if you scratch under the surface, you'll realize they are probably quite similar".

[88] David Vinuesa. "Carlos Moyá, entrenador de Nadal: 'Si el ego de Rafa fuese grande no nos escucharía como lo hace.'" *Libertad Digital*. Nov. 28, 2020. https://www.libertaddigital.com/deportes/tenis/2020-11-28/carlos-moya-entrenador-de-nadal-si-el-ego-de-rafa-fuese-grande-no-nos-escucharia-como-lo-hace-6685073/

[89] Daniel Moxon. "Rafael Nadal and Roger Federer's Relationship behind the Scenes Explained." *Express*. Feb. 5, 2022. https://www.express.co.uk/sport/tennis/1561568/Rafael-Nadal-Roger-Federer-relationship-tennis-news

Letting yourself be inspired by your rival represents the highest level of InQ.

Brené Brown: Researcher

Brené Brown was born in San Antonio, Texas, in the year 1965. She is an American research professor, lecturer, author, and podcast host[90]. Like most people who follow Brené Brown today, I was captivated by her 2010 TED Talk "The Power of Vulnerability"[91].

Until then, especially in corporate environments, vulnerability was not a trait anyone should have. But Brené brought a completely different perspective, showing vulnerability as an advantage in working environments and in your personal life. This concept transformed the whole leadership concept in the Western Hemisphere, making us understand a leader who is not vulnerable cannot inspire anyone.

As I have been so transformed by her research, I have followed her closely, listening to many of her conferences, and also many hours of her "Dare to Lead" podcast.

There are three reasons I think Brené is an inspirable person. The first is related to the story of her research for "The Power of Vulnerability", where she narrates all the difficulties to accept the unexpected findings she got from tons of interviews

---

[90] "Brené Brown." *Wikipedia*. Accessed June 13, 2022.
https://en.wikipedia.org/w/index.php?title=Bren%C3%A9_Brown&oldid=109 2951054

[91] Brené Brown. "The Power of Vulnerability." TEDxHouston. December 2010. Accessed July 20, 2022.
https://www.ted.com/talks/brene_brown_the_power_of_vulnerability?languag e=en

showing that the capacity to be vulnerable was the core enabler of empathizing, loving, and connecting with others.

The second reason I found listening to her podcasts. Similar to what I witnessed in Lewis Howes's "School of Greatness" podcast, I realized Brené was actually learning and enjoying most of the interviews. You can easily see how all these interactions have been sources of inspiration for her writing 6 New York Times bestsellers.

The third reason is her focus on her personal growth and humbleness. I'm not talking about all the academic degrees that she holds, but about her decision at one point in her life to leave all her addictions behind and start living a healthier life. Her openness and humbleness are powerful indicators of an inspirable person.

Gustavo Dudamel: Orchestra conductor

Gustavo Dudamel is the music director of Los Angeles Philharmonic, the Simón Bolívar Symphony Orchestra, and the Paris Opera. He was born in Venezuela in year 1981. His father was a trombonist and his mother a voice teacher. He began violin lessons as a child but was drawn to conduct from an early age. In 1999, at 18, he was appointed music director of the Simón Bolívar Youth Symphony Orchestra of Venezuela, composed of graduates of the El Sistema program[92].

---

[92] "El Sistema" (The System) was a social initiative created by Musician José Antonio Araujo in Venezuela in the year 1975 and provided after-school free music education and instrument usage to the participants who were mostly coming from low-income families. It is estimated that to date more than 700,000 students have benefited from this initiative.

Since then, he has become one of the most decorated conductors of his generation worldwide. When I started following his career, his achievements impressed me, of course, but as an observer looking for inspirable people, the language he used to describe his work piqued my interest.

Listening to one of his many interviews[93], he explained his job as connecting all the energies and thoughts in the orchestra to deliver a brilliant performance.

"

> "It is about convincing and let yourself be convinced, a dance, until you get to an agreement (...) The dialogue that happens in every rehearsal creates collective leadership, and I become just one more team member (...) the musician has to be a good listener, this is the key to transform cacophony into harmony."

There are many reasons to believe that Gustavo Dudamel is an inspirable person. His family of musicians inspired him, and as a conductor, he really became aware of the importance of connecting with everyone in the orchestra, which is one of the fundamental traits of the inspirable leader. Also, the openness reflected in the way he narrates the conversation that happens within the orchestra during each performance and the importance of listening are core attributes of the inspirable person.

---

[93] "Gustavo Dudamel, Director de Orquesta: Si El Mundo Funcionase Como Una Orquesta Habría Más Armonía." *Telefónica*. July 27,2021. https://www.youtube.com/watch?v=KzE5yGm5O5s

Melati and Isabel Wijsen: Activists

Melati Wijsen (born 2000) and Isabel Wijsen (born Nov. 6, 2002) are Indonesian climate activists. The two sisters are known for their efforts to reduce plastic consumption in Bali. In 2013 when they were only 12 and 10 years old, they kicked off their initiative to get rid of single-use plastic bags in Bali, which they called it Bye Bye Plastic Bags[94].

What ignited the inspirable spark in the Wijsen sisters? First, as they explained in a TED Talk[95] in 2016, they studied in an environmentally friendly school in Indonesia called Green School Valley, which created an important awareness in relation to the damage we are doing to our planet. More importantly, they were "taught to be the leaders of today." During one special class, they learned about the lives of inspirational leaders such as Lady Diana and Nelson Mandela. Later that day they decided they did not want to wait until they grew up to generate a significant impact, and that's how the idea was born.

What was the first thing they did? They identified their tribe of like-minded students from local and international students, and together they started an awareness campaign all over the island. Two years later they went to India, and they visited the place that used to be Mahatma Gandhi's home. His story inspired them to go on a hunger strike in Bali until the governor agreed to meet them, just 24 hours after their strike started. The

---

[94] "Bye Bye Plastic Bags – Say No To Plastic Bags." Accessed July 26, 2022. https://www.byebyeplasticbags.org/
[95] Melati and Isabel Wijsen. "Our Campaign to Ban Plastic Bags in Bali." TEDGlobal>London. January 2016.
https://www.ted.com/talks/melati_and_isabel_wijsen_our_campaign_to_ban_plastic_bags_in_bali

governor agreed to sign a full ban on single-use plastic bags in 2018.

Later they founded Youthtopia[96] a platform for young changemakers that supports many initiatives around the world to create a better place for the future. Youthtopia is led by young people, but they are inspirable enough to be mentored by who they call their circle of wisdom, a group of senior activists with experiences supporting noble causes around the world. The definition of Youthtopia's mission is an example of an Inspirable Organization:

“

"Youthtopia provides space that brings young people together, ignites their passions, and grows their skills to become active changemakers. This will be done by creating short & meaningful peer-to-peer programs guided by the 17 Sustainable Development Goals. These programs are made by the frontline young changemakers for the rising young change maker. For youth by youth."

Reading about Melati and Isabel's lives and initiatives, watching their videos, and listening to the interviews, I heard them so many times mention the countless sources of inspiration they had. This is something you can only do when you are an inspirable person. I inevitably compared their language with the one used by Rafael Nadal, Brené Brown, and Gustavo Dudamel. I found so many similarities that it

---

[96] "YOUTHTOPIA – a Platform for Young Changemakers."
https://youthtopia.world/

reaffirmed my conclusion: We are born inspirable, and even if we lose it on the way, we can always bring it back.

Appendix B - Inspirational reading and other sources

This book is a result of my experiences interacting and supporting the evolution of many organizations and workplaces. There is also a lot of wisdom here from the people in my tribe that dedicate their lives to propel the progression of tribes worldwide. Last but not least, this is the outcome of so many readings that gave me different solutions to the challenges of developing people and organizations in fast-changing environments. Here I would like to share those who have inspired me the most and the reason they did.

Atomic Habits*: An Easy & Proven Way to Build Good Habits & Break Bad Ones* by James Clear

James Clear, one of the world's leading experts on habit formation, reveals practical strategies that will teach you exactly how to form good habits and get rid of bad ones. Clear belongs to the new wave of authors who believe change should not be painful but requires discipline. His approach is all about initiating small actions, so tiny that he calls them atomic actions, which are the opposite of "be bold and ambitious" that we see in older methods.

I, Robot by Isaac Asimov.

For any sci-fi enthusiast, Asimov is a semi-god, and "I, Robot" his opera prima. This is the book where Asimov introduced his famous Three Laws of Robotic, which now, over 70 years after its first publishing, are still used as a reference for coding complex artificial intelligence applications, such as autonomous driving. His visions of the future where robots provide immense possibilities to humankind, and the dilemmas we need to face, ignited my interest in people's development at a very early age.

Indistractable: How to Control Your Attention and Choose Your Life by Nir Eyal

This is a book about focus, setting your priorities, and starting from yourself. Distraction is doing something without intention. It has plenty of tips to manage the distractions that are coming from the digital space. Nir provides many lessons about how to stay in the present. He is also similar to most contemporary gurus and is against multitasking.

Immunity to Change: How to Overcome It and Unlock Potential in Yourself and Your Organization by Lisa Laskow Lahey and Robert Kegan

For coaching lovers, this is my favorite approach. If you follow the structure proposed, you will help your clients get unstuck quickly. I think this method is for people who already know what they want but something is holding them back. It works for individuals and groups. It is a traditional method in the sense that is not tribe-based, but it is painless as the change process starts very modest and it grows slowly.

Reinventing   Organizations*: A Guide to Creating Organizations Inspired by the Next Stage in Human Consciousness* by Frederic Laloux

It is always useful to have a roadmap, and in terms of organizational culture evolution, this is a very good one. The description of the different cultural stages, from the authority-driven ones to the collaboratives, is a great tool to diagnose the health of corporations. The reason I liked this book is that in the final stage, the Teal culture represents a lot of the values needed in Inspirable Organizations, or maybe it's the other way around: having inspirable people is a must in a Teal organization.

Start With Why*: How Great Leaders Inspire Everyone to Take Action* by Simon Sinek

Having a purpose is one of the most powerful drivers for women and men. This concept captured me when I first read Viktor Frankl's *Man's Search for Meaning*. Sinek brings this concept to life again in the context of organizations in the 21st century. It struck me to realize how often we focus on "what" we are doing, not knowing "why" we are doing it.

The 100-Year Life*: Living and Working in an Age of Longevity* by Lynda Gratton and Andrew Scott

This book describes the challenges we are going to face as our lives get longer. It has a special focus on our working life. We might work for 50 or 60 years before we retire, so we need a plan. The solution is about building 3 types of intangible assets: productivity, relationships, and transformational ones. This book had an important impact on how I was planning my life and development, but most importantly, how I could support my daughter's development as she is supposed to live even longer than I.

The Future of Professions*: How Technology Will Transform the Work of Human Experts* by Richard Susskind and Daniel Susskind

It is a book about the decline of today's professions. What I found most interesting was the reasons for this decline, these could be our compass to rethink the professions of the future, and act as a guide for our own long-term development.

The Gap and the Gain*: The High Achievers' Guide to Happiness, Confidence, and Success* by Daniel Sullivan and Benjamin Hardy

As a corporate animal, I was used to focusing on achieving goals, and I was also often frustrated by not achieving them. Even when accomplishing them, I did not celebrate enough because another goal was waiting around the corner. Reading this book energized me by helping me focus on the gains and showing me how to compare myself with who I was that day or the year before. In conclusion, it helped me set a measuring system for my growth.

The Good Life: Lessons from the World's Longest Scientific Study of Happiness by Robert Waldinger and Marc Schulz.

This book is the result of a study conducted for more than 80 years by Harvard University. The analysis of tons of data obtained over decades concludes that there is only one common variable that contributes significantly to having a good life: the development of personal relationships. This finding definitely indicates that the model presented in this book is on the right track. I recommend reading it, because beyond data, the book shows many personal stories that can inspire us to make "tweaks" in our lives.

***The Network Always Wins**: How to Influence Customers, Stay Relevant, and Transform Your Organization to Move Faster than the Market* by Peter Hinssen

In today's fast-moving marketplace, networks are power. This book shows you how to harness that power. For me, the key value that I got from this book is the understanding that in our current times with most of the problems that we face, the network solves them quicker than the individual. So, it makes no sense to be struggling by ourselves or with our small team to figure out a solution. We need to connect first. Does this sound familiar?

The Power of Vulnerability: TEDxHouston, by Brené Brown

A few years ago, leaders used to provide directions, listen to their teams, and include their feedback on the plan. Leaders were flawless and managed their own development areas discretely. Brené Brown introduced a novel concept: Leaders need to be vulnerable, and this not only will be helpful for their development but will also be positive for the engagement of the tribe.

The School of Greatness (podcast) by Lewis Howes

I listen to this podcast on a weekly basis. Most of the authors that have inspired this book have been guests on the show. Its host, Lewis Howes, makes the interviews entertaining but also keeps them focused on the important subjects and doesn't avoid any difficult discussion.

The three-body problem trilogy by Cixin Liu.

Timelines in Liu's books stretch for millions of years, showing incredible scenarios for our hungry minds. With scientific precision, he shows us that everything is changing in the surrounding universe, and our societies have to act together to make sure that we prevail. His view is not an endogamic one, where everything that happens to us is a consequence of our actions, even though his work has a powerful message about the way we treat our home planet.

Thinking, fast and slow by Daniel Kahneman

It took me around three months to read this book and absorb every experiment, its conclusions, and the impact of those findings on how we understand human behavior. It is a must-read for any professional who wants to lead or support change of any kind. Kahneman reshaped everything we knew about decision-making, earning him the Nobel Prize in Economic Sciences.

Tribal Leadership: *Leveraging Natural Groups to Build a Thriving Organization* by Dave Logan, John King and Halee Fischer-Wright

The concept of the tribe that is used in this book is one I can easily relate to, as I have witnessed it in every organization I have been in contact with. What I love about this book is the concrete approach to identifying the stage your tribe and a straightforward way to develop it with many suggestions, tips, and actions.

Tribes: *We Need You to Lead Us* by Seth Godin

This book focuses on the tribe concept proposed in the Tribal Leadership book, but it is more oriented to clients, sales, and marketing than to organizations. The most important value of this book is its capacity to inspire. After reading it, I got a tremendous energy shot to start moving and contribute to the paradigm shift that needs to happen in the business world.

Acknowledgment

The making of this book taught me a lesson: I will never know the limits of people's generosity. I want to thank many of you for your contributions to this endeavor.

I want to thank my wife Bleric for her support during this inspiring journey, for her full engagement with the writing of this book, her endless reviews, honest feedback, kind suggestions, and for coping with my extended periods of reflection, silence, and grumpiness. This book would not exist without you.

I want to thank my draft readers: Andrés Cardona, Daniel Vanegas, and again, my wife Bleric. Your patience helped transform a succession of ideas into a story and a framework that hopefully makes sense.

Thanks to L.A. Eaton for kick-starting the book with me. After many conversations, you helped me transform the ideas that I had in mind into a series of chapters. Thanks to Bethany McKay for your final review of this document, ensuring the flow and the readability that was lacking in my non-native English writing. Thanks to Nisha Dorch for representing visually what Inspirable means and designing a cover that I love.

During the creation of this book, I had many conversations with special people: Cassidy Edwards, Neringa Kalpokas, Navid Nazemian, Deborah Hartung, and Pedro Fernández. Your contributions are all over the book. Thank you.

I am grateful to the leaders that lit my way: Jorge Davyt, Ginette Martin, Miguel Bolinaga, Wim Focquet, Pedro Muñoz, Haider

Imam, Mahmoud Sobh, Sofía Víctor, Michael Skovsgaard, Morten Kongsbak, Luis González Llobet, David González Llobet, Victoria Alcober, Marcos Málaga, Eduardo Cabrera, Javier Martin de la Fuente, José Manuel Arribas, Laura Fernández, Carmen Martin, Maria Grazia Mazzaro, and Enrique Aguirre.

Thank you to all my students at IE University. Your ideas have inspired me every year. I'm proud and happy to know that you are the people that will be in charge very soon.

A big thank you to my family: my mom, my dad, and my brother. Belonging to this small tribe made life for me a lot easier.

And finally, thank you, dear reader, for taking your time reading this book. It means the world to me.

August 2022

Index

STAY INSPIRABLE

WWW.BEINSPIRABLE.COM

DANLAYAQ

www.ingramcontent.com/pod-product-compliance
Lightning Source LLC
Chambersburg PA
CBHW050440290526
45786CB00006B/2102